Welcome to England Women's Football Legends

Lunar Press is a privately-run publishing company that cares greatly about its content's accuracy.

If you notice any inaccuracies or have anything that you would like to discuss in the book, then please email us at lunarpresspublishers@gmail.com.

Enjoy!

© Copyright 2024 - All rights reserved.
The content contained within this book may not be reproduced, duplicated or transmitted without direct written permission from the author or the publisher.

Under no circumstances will any blame or legal responsibility be held against the publisher, or author, for any damages, reparation, or monetary loss due to the information contained within this book, either directly or indirectly.

Legal Notice:
This book is copyright protected. It is only for personal use. You cannot amend, distribute, sell, use, quote or paraphrase any part, or the content within this book, without the consent of the author or publisher.

Disclaimer Notice:
Please note the information contained within this document is for educational and entertainment purposes only. All effort has been executed to present accurate, up to date, reliable, complete information. No warranties of any kind are declared or implied. Readers acknowledge that the author is not engaged in the rendering of legal, financial, medical or professional advice. The content within this book has been derived from various sources. Please consult a licensed professional before attempting any techniques outlined in this book.

By reading this document, the reader agrees that under no circumstances is the author responsible for any losses, direct or indirect, that are incurred as a result of the use of the information contained within this document, including, but not limited to, errors, omissions, or inaccuracies.

CONTENTS

Jill Scott	7
Kelly Smith	13
Marieanne Spacey	18
Lucy Bronze	23
Gillian Coulthard	29
Nikita Parris	34
Alex Greenwood	40
Mary Earps	45
Alex Scott	51
Carol Thomas	56
Casey Stoney	61
Rachel Yankey	66
Fara Williams	71
Steph Houghton	77
Sheila Parker	82
Ellen White	87
Karen Carney	92
Fran Kirby	97
Leah Williamson	102
Beth Mead	107

KICK OFF

As you read this book, you will quickly see that just about every woman in it has an MBE* or some other form of exceptional recognition. That's because all of them have had to work harder to get to the top than any male footballer in history. Why? Because up until the late 2010s, women's football got little to no coverage. The players were (and still are) paid a lot less, and most of the time, they were considered amateurs.

Respect for the women's game has improved a great deal in recent years, but the general public still has a lot to learn about how high the standard really is. For everyone who watched Euro 2022 and that wonderful Lionesses victory, or the 2023 World Cup when they came so close, we know that the women's game is pure class. It's just a shame so many people don't know this yet.

Of course, there are many other world-class female footballers who aren't English, such as Sam Kerr, Aitana Bonmati and Alexandra Popp, but our goal in this book is to take a look at the Lionesses who changed the game. Players such as Jill Scott, Mary Earps and Lucy Bronze. And others you might not have heard of, like Carol Thomas and Sheila Parker, the "woman who started it all"!

You will also notice that the entrants haven't been

numbered. That's because it is almost impossible to decide who is number one and who isn't. Every player here has earned their place, and all for different reasons. Who is the greatest Lioness of all time? Well, that's a matter of opinion, and that's also the beauty of sports: It's up to you to decide who you think is best!

All of the women who make it at the top level of football deserve our respect. And it's a wonderful thing that some of that respect is finally starting to be shown. Never has there been more Women's Super League (WSL) games live on TV, and the 2023 World Cup brought in more viewers than ever before. With each season, new records are being broken, and the old, unfair views are changing.

Along with the skills, goals, wonder saves, tackles and determination of the 20 women in this book come their struggles. Struggles against discrimination, online abuse and even hatred. The stars of women's football have a lot more negativity to deal with than the men, yet they always carry themselves with their heads held high.

When you read about Rachel Yankey having to shave her head at age 8 just so she could stay on the boys' team, then you will start to understand how unfair the rules can be for the girls. Or maybe it will be the story of Fara Williams, who was still sleeping on the streets even as she made her senior England debut.

But this book isn't all about hardships; it's also about celebrating greatness. Our 20 superstars have won just about everything there is to win, including countless Champions Leagues, Euros, WSL titles, doubles, trebles and even a few quadruples! These are the greatest Lionesses and domestic stars of all time. They are legends of the English game. And their stories are all here for you to enjoy!

JILL SCOTT MBE

TEAMS

SUNDERLAND
2004–2006
↓
EVERTON
2006–2013
APPS – 114, GLS – 21
↓
MANCHESTER CITY
2013–2022
APPS – 111, GLS – 19
↓
EVERTON (LOAN)
2021
APPS – 11, GLS – 2
↓
ASTON VILLA (LOAN)
2022
APPS – 7, GLS – 0

TROPHY CABINET

EUROS	X1
WSL	X1
FA CUP	X4
NATIONAL LEAGUE CUP	X1
FA LEAGUE CUP	X3

ENGLAND STATS

CAPS	GOALS
161	27

BIOGRAPHY

BORN	2ND FEB 1987
POSITION(S)	MIDFIELDER
STRONG FOOT	RIGHT
RETIRED	2022
HEIGHT	5 FT 11 IN (1.81 M)

First, we will start with a player who played an unbelievable 161 times for her country. With her tall frame and stamina, Jill Scott became one of the most dynamic midfielders in the women's game. Apart from her hugely successful England career, in which she won the 2022 Euros, she also had a great club career, playing mainly for Everton and Manchester City.

Jill Scott was born in Sunderland on the 2nd of February, 1987. As a child, she showed her athletic ability early, and her parents pretty much knew she was destined for a life in sports. But football wasn't her only passion. Jill was a fantastic long-distance runner, winning the Under-13 North of England cross-country title in the Junior Great North Run when she was just 12!

Her love of long-distance running helped build her stamina, so by the time she was playing for her local team, Bolden Girls, she was the fittest player on the pitch by a long shot. It helped her develop her all-action midfield style, and it allowed her to play box-to-box for the full 90 minutes without ever losing any of her sharpness.

When Jill hit her teens, she was told that if she wanted to be a top-level athlete when she grew up, she might have to choose between football and running and concentrate solely on one. Thankfully for the

Lionesses and women's football as a whole, she picked football.

That Bolden team Jill played for were unstoppable. They won everything. It's not surprising, though, since two of Jill's teammates, Demi Stokes and Steph Houghton, were future England players. We will cover Steph later in this book. She is another footballing legend!

Jill finished school in 2003 and studied exercise science at Gateshead College. While there, she continued to develop her footballing talents. After Gateshead, she finished her diploma at the University of Sunderland. By the time she was done, she felt like she was ready to take the next step in her professional football career.

Her local club, Sunderland, had spotted her talents early on. She was signed on youth terms while she was in college, and after a rapid rise through the Under-19s, Jill was well on her way to the top. She won several youth awards, which brought her to the attention of Everton, a team famed in the women's game for getting the best out of their young players.

Jill signed for the Toffees* in 2005, having never made a first-team appearance for Sunderland (she was still only 17). She was quickly thrown into the deep end at Everton, making her senior debut against the mighty Arsenal in the Community Shield. Arsenal were (and still are) the most dominant team in the history of the Women's Premier League, which was the name of the top division in England before it changed to the WSL in 2010.

Jill's first game ended in defeat, but she had a taste for the big occasion, and she wanted more.

Her early performances for Everton were fantastic, and she was soon being called up to the England squad. She made her debut only a few months after playing her first game for Everton, coming on as a substitute against Holland. But her rapid rise didn't end there, and Jill was called up to the England squad for the 2007 World Cup!

After starting the opening group game against Japan on the bench, Jill came on in the second half and bossed it. In fact, she played so well that she was given a start in the next game and kept her place for the rest of the tournament. One of her highlights was scoring her first England goal in a 6–0 demolition of Argentina.

England went out in the quarter-finals after losing to international giants America, but the tournament was seen as a massive success. More people than ever were watching women's football, and the Lionesses' brilliant showing had millions of young girls around Britain believing they could be superstars. Still, there was a long way to go before it was as popular as it is today.

Jill's second season as a pro was amazing. Not only did she help Everton win the League Cup in 2008, but she was also named the Football Association (FA) Players' Player of the Year! But that final wasn't just any old victory. Everton had never won a major trophy before, and they were playing Arsenal, the greatest team in the women's game. Everton shocked the nation with their win, and it gave them their first trophy. It was Jill's first of many, too!

And Everton's underdog story wasn't finished there. Two years later, they reached the FA Cup final, an even bigger competition than the League Cup. Again, they faced Arsenal, a team that had won the FA Cup in the four previous seasons and were looking to make it five in a row! To make it even more of a challenge, Arsenal were playing in their tenth FA Cup final, having won every single one of them!

Everton won a cracking match in extra time, the game finishing 3–2 in what is considered one of the greatest FA Cup finals of all time. If you haven't seen it before, look it up on YouTube! You won't be disappointed.

By this point, most of the world's biggest teams were chasing Jill. She stayed loyal to Everton for a few more years but eventually signed for up-and-coming Manchester City in 2013. Two years before that, she starred for England at the 2011 World Cup. Despite netting in a win over New Zealand earlier in the tournament, England crashed out at the quarter-final stage again.

Her time at City was massively successful, and she won the League Cup in 2014 and again in 2016. The second of these was made even more special by the fact that City lifted their first (and Jill's first) WSL trophy.

Three FA Cups and a couple more League Cups followed, and as Jill winded down her career, she spent some time on loan at her old club Everton and had a short stint at Aston Villa.

Jill made her 150th appearance for England in 2021, a year after being given her MBE. She followed this up by helping the Lionesses to their proudest moment—lifting the 2022 European Championship. Jill was a veteran by then, and she was used sparingly throughout the tournament, but her experience was priceless.

She retired soon after and has moved into TV work, which she is a natural at. Jill has also spent her career fighting for LGBTQ+ rights, and she is proudly and openly gay.

A true legend of the English game, there haven't been many box-to-box midfielders in the class of Jill Scott!

of many, too!

And Everton's underdog story wasn't finished there. Two years later, they reached the FA Cup final, an even bigger competition than the League Cup. Again, they faced Arsenal, a team that had won the FA Cup in the four previous seasons and were looking to make it five in a row! To make it even more of a challenge, Arsenal were playing in their tenth FA Cup final, having won every single one of them!

Everton won a cracking match in extra time, the game finishing 3–2 in what is considered one of the greatest FA Cup finals of all time. If you haven't seen it before, look it up on YouTube! You won't be disappointed.

By this point, most of the world's biggest teams were chasing Jill. She stayed loyal to Everton for a few more years but eventually signed for up-and-coming Manchester City in 2013. Two years before that, she starred for England at the 2011 World Cup. Despite netting in a win over New Zealand earlier in the tournament, England crashed out at the quarter-final stage again.

Her time at City was massively successful, and she won the League Cup in 2014 and again in 2016. The second of these was made even more special by the fact that City lifted their first (and Jill's first) WSL trophy.

Three FA Cups and a couple more League Cups followed, and as Jill winded down her career, she spent some time on loan at her old club Everton and had a short stint at Aston Villa.

Jill made her 150th appearance for England in 2021, a year after being given her MBE. She followed this up by helping the Lionesses to their proudest moment—lifting the 2022 European Championship. Jill was a veteran by then, and she was used sparingly throughout the tournament, but her experience was priceless.

She retired soon after and has moved into TV work, which she is a natural at. Jill has also spent her career fighting for LGBTQ+ rights, and she is proudly and openly gay.

A true legend of the English game, there haven't been many box-to-box midfielders in the class of Jill Scott!

KELLY SMITH MBE

TEAMS

WEMBLEY LADIES
1994–1996
↓
ARSENAL
1996–1997
↓
NEW JERSEY LADY STALLIONS
1999–2000
↓
PHILADELPHIA CHARGE
2001–2003
APPS – 26, GLS – 9
↓
NEW JERSEY WILDCATS
2004
APPS – 8, GLS – 8
↓
ARSENAL
2005–2009
APPS – 66, GLS – 73
↓
BOSTON BREAKERS
2009–2012
APPS – 46, GLS – 18
↓
ARSENAL
2012–2017
APPS – 23, GLS – 9

TROPHY CABINET

WOMEN'S PREMIER LEAGUE	X5
FA CUP	X5
NATIONAL LEAGUE CUP	X1
FA COMMUNITY SHIELD	X3
CHAMPIONS LEAGUE	X1
CYPRUS CUP	X1

ENGLAND STATS

CAPS	GOALS
117	46

BIOGRAPHY

BORN	29TH OCT 1978
POSITION(S)	STRIKER
STRONG FOOT	LEFT
RETIRED	2017
HEIGHT	5 FT 6 IN (1.68 M)

Kelly Smith is one of the players we can safely say helped to put women's football on the map. She is an Arsenal legend as well as an all-time England great who won every domestic honour, including five league titles. Kelly is one of the most natural finishers to ever play the game, and despite several serious injuries, she still managed to play for her country 117 times.

Born on the 29th of October, 1978, in Watford, Kelly grew up in the Garston area of the city. Her love of football was there from the beginning, and at a time when there weren't many girls' teams for kids to play on, she usually turned out for the boys. It was said that she was always the best player on the pitch by a mile.

She was so good that during one season for the boys' Under-8s, she was kicked off the team after parents of the other players complained. Of course, they used the excuse that she was a girl and the team was meant to be for boys, but everyone knew it was just because Kelly was too good.

Kelly was removed from the team halfway through the season, yet she still ended up being the top scorer!

After leaving the boys' team, Kelly joined Pinner Girls, a team started by her father, who was sick of the silly rules stopping his kid from playing organised football. The team was made up of Kelly's cousins, friends and other local girls. They were fantastic!

She spent her youth career with Wembley Ladies and made her senior debut at just 16! A year later, Kelly was a full England international. Her England debut was amazing for a couple of reasons. Of course, it was impressive because she was just 17, but Kelly also won Player of the Match. Her performances that season led to her being included in England's squad for the 1995 World Cup, but she couldn't travel with the team as she had to sit her GCSEs!

Kelly's goal-scoring talents were evident early on, and it took only two England games before she netted the first of many for her country.

Her rise was rapid, and when Arsenal came calling, she decided to leave Wembley Ladies after two great years. As we've mentioned before, Arsenal were the best team in the country by far, but this was before the Premier League became the WSL. Women's football in England was still a bit behind Europe and, especially, America. Kelly wanted to test herself against the best, and she decided that a move to the USA would be best for her development.

Before that, she won the first of many major tournaments at club level when Arsenal lifted the league title in 1997. In the title-winning game against Liverpool, Kelly scored two and made one. It was the perfect send-off before her move to America.

She spent five years in the States, playing for the New Jersey Lady Stallions, Philadelphia Charge and the New Jersey Wildcats. Kelly was still in college when she left Arsenal, and she continued her studies at Seton Hall University. She also played college soccer there and broke pretty much every record at that level.

After her time in America was up, Kelly returned to England and her beloved Arsenal. It was during this period that she would make her name as one of the best finishers (and one of the best players) of all time. She signed in time for the 2005–06 season but wasn't fit to start, having suffered a serious leg break near the end of her time in the States. When she finally made her second Arsenal debut, she broke her foot a few minutes into it and had to spend several more months on the sidelines.

She recovered in time for the run-in and scored another title-winning goal, this time a 30-yard screamer that is still remembered today.

That same year, she played so well in a World Cup qualifier against Holland that their coach, Mia Hamm, described Kelly as the greatest player in the world. Many sports pundits and fellow players agreed.

The 2006–07 season was massive, as Arsenal won the quadruple, including the UEFA Women's Cup. Kelly scored an impressive 30 goals in 34 games. She spent four years with Arsenal during her second spell but left to return to America when a new, more professional league was being created. Kelly signed with the Boston Breakers, and she was quickly followed across the Atlantic by many English players who were sick of the low standards of pay and facilities back home.

Kelly was one of the stars of England's brilliant effort

at the 2009 Euros, scoring three goals. The Lionesses just fell short, losing to Germany in the final after some wonderful performances.

The 2011 World Cup saw the Lionesses play well again, only to lose a tight quarter-final on penalties against France. The game itself had finished 1-1, with Kelly scoring England's goal.

After three years with the Boston Breakers, Kelly rejoined Arsenal for a third time. It wasn't the fairy tale return she hoped for, and her time there was blighted by injuries. She only managed 23 games in five years.

Kelly retired from international football in 2015 and club football two years later. Despite her career being filled with injuries, she still managed to score regularly whenever and wherever she played. She was in the final voting for the World Player of the Year award four times, finishing third in 2009, fourth in 2007 and fifth in 2006 and 2008.

When any list of the best finishers of all time (both men and women) is made, Kelly Smith has to be near the top.

MARIEANNE SPACEY

Teams

FRIENDS OF FULHAM
1982-1993
↓
ROI LAZIO
1985
↓
HJK HELSINKI
1989
↓
ARSENAL
1993-2002
↓
FULHAM
2002-2005

Trophy Cabinet

WOMEN'S PREMIER LEAGUE	X4
FA CUP	X5
NATIONAL LEAGUE CUP	X7
FA INTERNATIONAL PLAYER OF THE YEAR	X2

England Stats

CAPS	GOALS
91	28

BIOGRAPHY

BORN	13TH FEB 1966
BIRTHPLACE	SUTTON
POSITION(S)	CAM / CF
RETIRED	2005
HEIGHT	N/A

Once again, we have another attacking superstar, but unlike Kelly Smith who was an out-and-out poacher, Marieanne Spacey could also play a more creative role. Her ability to shift between a number 9 and a 10 made her a nightmare for defenders, and even at a time when women's football was in its infancy, she still managed to become a household name.

Marieanne played 91 times for the Lionesses, and since her retirement, she has done a lot of work for better facilities, opportunities and standards in girls' football. She is currently the Head of Women's & Girls Football at Southampton, where she is also the team's coach!

Born in Sutton, London, on the 13th of February, 1966, Marieanne grew up with little opportunity to play organised football. The boys' teams were off-limits for girls back then, so she had to settle for kickabouts in the local fields and pitches. Whenever she did play with the boys, she was the best player by far.

By the time she was in her teens, a few girls' teams had started to crop up in Britain. There was nothing like there is today, but at least it was a start. Marieanne joined the British Oxygen women's team at just 13 and instantly became their best player despite lining up alongside adults.

She was spotted by scouts for Friends of Fulham*, and

their manager, Fred Brockwell, signed her up. Back then, all women's football was amateur or part-time at best. Sadly, it stayed that way for a long time, and it's only been in recent years that we've begun to see the women's game getting the respect it deserves.

Marieanne signed a part-time contract with Friends of Fulham, and she was still working a regular job when she made her England debut against Belgium in 1984. It didn't take her long to become a regular starter, and it was quickly realised that she was England's best player.

Despite her early success, Marieanne was struggling to maintain her football career while also having to work full-time. At one point, she thought she would have to hang up her boots, but her love for the game was too much.

One of her England teammates, Louise Waller, often travelled to Finland in the summer to play in their league. The women's Finnish league was a summer competition, and it paid pretty well, which meant top players like Marieanne could go there for three months, play, and be back in time for the English season!

Before her first stint in Finland, Marieanne had the small matter of an FA Cup final to contend with. It was her first taste of the big time, and she loved it, despite Fulham's 3–2 loss to Leasowe Pacific at Old Trafford. Following the game, she signed for HJK Helsinki for the summer league.

As soon as she returned from Finland, Marieanne was

thrown straight into the opening game of the 1991–92 season with Fulham, who had just recently changed their name to Wimbledon Women. She had no break in between, so it had been just constant football and work for over a year. It made no difference. Marieanne took off like a rocket, scoring an incredible 12 goals in the opening five games!

Soon, England's biggest teams were trying to sign her, and in 1993, she ended up signing for the biggest of them all—Arsenal. Her career continued to progress with the Gunners. Being surrounded by a better standard of player suited her, and she raised her game.

Marieanne was a major part of the England team that played in their first-ever World Cup in 1995. And she scored in England's first-ever World Cup game, a 3–2 win over Canada. The team performed admirably, going out in the quarter-finals to eventual finalists Germany.

She spent eight successful years at Arsenal, playing as an attacking midfielder or an out-and-out striker. Wherever she played, Marieanne always made a difference. Due to her standout performances, she became one of the first female players in the history of the English game to sign a professional contract. For this alone, she deserves her legendary status. She opened the door for all of the top players who have followed.

As her England career was winding down, she finished it by flying to Germany with the England team for the 2001 Euros. Unfortunately, the Lionesses didn't perform well and went out in the group stage.

Marieanne was 36, and she was starting to feel that her international career was coming to an end.

Her final season with Arsenal saw her finish as the league's top scorer despite her age. She was given the Players' Player of the Year award as well as a Sport Relief special achievement award. In her time with the Gunners, she won all there was to win domestically. At 36, people expected her to retire, but she moved to Fulham (not her old team, but the Fulham we know today), where things were about to get crazy!

Marieanne's first season with Fulham might actually be the most impressive of her career. With a team that wasn't expected to do much, she led them to the league, the FA Cup and the League Cup in what was a memorable treble! Oh, and she was 37 at the time!

She retired a couple of years later and began her career developing the women's game in England. Since then, she's moved into coaching but continues to work with local communities and the FA to improve the standards of girls' and women's football.

As a player, Marieanne Spacey was often compared to Arsenal legend Dennis Bergkamp. They both played as a number 10, and they both had an eye for goal. I think it's safe to say that any player who gets compared to Bergkamp must have been good! Marieanne Spacey certainly was one of the best!

LUCY BRONZE MBE

Teams

SUNDERLAND
2007–2010
APPS – 25, GLS – 5

↓

EVERTON
2010–2012
APPS – 20, GLS – 2

↓

LIVERPOOL
2012–2014
APPS – 28, GLS – 3

↓

MANCHESTER CITY
2014–2017
APPS – 34, GLS – 5

↓

LYON
2017–2020
APPS – 50, GLS – 3

↓

MANCHESTER CITY
2020–2022
APPS – 31, GLS – 2

↓

BARCELONA
2022–
APPS – 34, GLS – 3

Trophy Cabinet

EUROS	X1
WSL	X3
FA LEAGUE CUP	X2
FA CUP	X2
CHAMPIONS LEAGUE	X4
D1 FEMININE	X3
LIGA F	X1

England Stats

CAPS	GOALS
119	15

BIOGRAPHY

BORN	28TH OCT 1991
POSITION(S)	RB / RWB
STRONG FOOT	RIGHT
RETIRED	STILL PLAYING
HEIGHT	5 FT 8 IN (1.72 M)

At just 32 at the time of this book being written and having won pretty much everything there is to win in the game, it's scary to think how many medals Lucy Bronze will have when she finally hangs up her boots. But it's not just her trophy cabinet that she'll be remembered for. Lucy is one of the most naturally gifted players in the history of the sport. A talented right-back who can attack and defend, she has developed into a modern-day inverted full-back who can drift into midfield and create from there, too.

Lucy Bronze was born in Berwick-upon-Tweed on the 28th of October, 1991, to a Portuguese father and an English mother. Because of this, she was raised bilingual*, which meant that as she grew older, learning new languages came quite easily to her. This helped her settle in quickly when she would later move abroad to play football.

A shy child, Lucy often found it hard to join in games of football around her estate and on the local pitches. But when she did build up the courage, her talents made her a popular figure in her hometown. With a right foot like a wand, she was a genius on the pitch. By the time she was 11, most of her shyness was gone, especially when she was playing football.

Lucy was the star player on the local boys' team, Belford. Soon after, she was asked to play for Alnwick

Town, who were the best team in the area. Sadly, she had to leave when she turned 12 due to the rule that girls couldn't play on the boys' teams once they became teenagers.

She was so good at Alnwick that in her first eight matches, she won six "Man" of the Match awards! Her coach actually tried to take the FA to court in the hopes that they would change the rule that stopped Lucy from playing on after turning 13!

Lucy also starred for her school's team in Alnwick, captaining them while also captaining their tennis and hockey teams. In her time at the Duchess's Community High School, she managed to win a county championship every year in at least one of the three sports! To top it off, Lucy was also an exceptional runner, and at one point, she was tipped to represent England in the 800 metres at the Olympics!

Despite her busy schedule (hockey, football, running and tennis take up a lot of time!), Lucy still managed to win a bronze medal at the National Mathematics Trust Challenge. It seems that she was blessed with both brains and sporting ability!

Sunderland signed her as a kid, and throughout her development, she played in a number of positions. She could run the game from midfield, often playing as a number 10, 8 or even a 6. But she usually ended up in her beloved right-back position.

The day she turned 16, Sunderland promoted her to the first team. Despite her young age, Lucy played most of that 2007–08 season, helping Sunderland win the Northern Division title and promotion to the top flight. An already successful season was made even better when they reached the FA Cup final, only narrowly losing 2–1 to Arsenal.

Oh, and Lucy managed all this while still attending school!

It wasn't long before the national team came calling, but not the one you might think! Portugal was the first country to approach her, and Lucy later admitted that she considered pledging her allegiance to her father's home nation. This had a lot to do with England taking their time in calling her up, but thankfully for the Lionesses, Lucy held out and the England coaches finally saw sense!

Lucy finished school at 17 and moved to America to continue her studies. She attended the University of North Carolina, where she also played for their team, the Tar Heels. She returned to England a year later to attend Leeds Metropolitan University, graduating in 2013 with a degree in sports science.

Throughout her time in college and even several years into her football career, Lucy had to work at Dominos to support herself. Little did she know that nearly a decade later, the pizza chain would use her image for adverts following England's wonderful win at Euro 2022!

With college out of the way, Lucy had her pick of clubs. Sunderland wanted to keep her, but Lucy had outgrown them. She was quickly becoming one of the best right-backs in the world. One of her old youth coaches from the England setup, Maureen "Mo" Marley, was working at Everton, and when she offered her the chance to join, Lucy took it.

But her time at Everton wasn't the best. Lucy suffered a lot of injuries, which stalled her progress. Playing in the newly formed WSL wasn't easy, as the standard had rapidly increased. Still, she played in the Champions League for the Toffees, which was an achievement in itself.

The WSL might have been bigger and better than the old Premier League, but most of the players were considered part-time. While Lucy was playing for Everton and England, she still had to keep working at Dominos. That's how unfair it was back then.

Lucy was part of the Everton exodus* that left to join bitter rivals Liverpool before the 2013 season when Liverpool became the first full-time women's team in England. Other players who joined included Fara Williams (who we will cover later) and Natasha Dowie. Lucy told reporters years later that one of the main reasons she joined Liverpool was because of their professional medical system, which helped her recover from her knee injuries.

Liverpool instantly won back-to-back WSL titles, with Lucy's performances earning her the 2014 Player of the Year award. Big-spending Manchester City came calling soon after, and Lucy decided to move on. Her year was complete when she played for England in the first-ever women's game at the new Wembley Stadium.

Lucy continued to suffer injuries, and when the 2015 World Cup rolled around, she had been replaced at right-back by Alex Scott. Still, Lucy was too good not to start, so she started in midfield. After a couple of games building her fitness, she replaced Scott at right-back for the rest of the tournament and scored a worldy in a 2–1 win over Norway. England lost in the semis, but Lucy was still named England's best player that year.

Lucy moved to Lyon in 2017, where she won the treble and the quadruple, including three Champions Leagues in as many seasons. She returned to City for another couple of years before making her dream move to Barcelona in 2022, where she quickly won the treble. She still currently plays there.

Of course, 2022 was a dream for another reason: that historical Euros win with the Lionesses! A disappointing loss in the final of the World Cup followed a year later, but who will be surprised if Lucy leads her country to more glory before her career ends?

Has there been a more complete right-back in the history of the women's game? Surely not.

GILLIAN COULTARD
MBE

Teams

DONCASTER ROVER BELLES
1976–1982

↓

ROWNTREE W.F.C.
1982–1986

↓

DONCASTER ROVER BELLES
1986–2001

Trophy Cabinet

WOMEN'S PREMIER LEAGUE	X2
FA CUP	X6
MUNDIALITO	X1

England Stats

CAPS	GOALS
119	30

BIOGRAPHY

BORN	22ND JULY 1963
BIRTHPLACE	THORNE
POSITION(S)	CDM / SWEEPER
RETIRED	2001
HEIGHT	5 FT 0 IN (1.52 M)

Gillian Coultard achieved many things in her wonderful career, but maybe the most impressive was when she became the first woman to win 100 caps for England. In fact, she was the fifth overall, after legendary men's players Peter Shilton, Sir Bobby Moore, Bobby Charlton and Billy Wright.

A defensive midfielder who could control the game, Gillian switched to sweeper in her later years but was just as effective. In her two spells with Doncaster Rovers Belles, she won the Premier League twice and the FA Cup on six occasions. In her life, she has fought and beat cancer, and she was inducted into the English Football Hall of Fame in 2006.

Oh, and she did all of this and more while also working on a construction line in a warehouse!

Born on the 22nd of July, 1963, Gillian grew up in a time of progress. The sixties and the seventies saw huge improvements in women's rights, but things were still very lopsided*, especially when it came to sports. And, in the small mining village in Doncaster where Gillian spent her childhood, girls were expected to grow up to be homemakers or, at most, secretaries. The idea that a girl might want to play football as a career was unheard of, but Gillian clearly didn't listen!

The youngest of eight children, Gillian was never short

of someone to play football with. Her older brothers took her along to the park for matches, where the other boys would go in extra hard on Gillian, trying to make her cry. It was in these rough-and-tumble matches that she developed her tough-tackling style. It wasn't long before she was giving the boys as much as they gave her!

Of course, as you will have seen already in this book, there came a stage when Gillian wasn't allowed to play on the boys' teams anymore, which broke her heart. With nobody to play with, one of her teachers (who knew how good Gillian was) told her to try out for the Doncaster Belles youth team. Gillian did, and the coaches were instantly impressed.

In fact, it wasn't just the Doncaster coaches who were blown away by Gillian's talents. Scouts from Europe soon heard about the all-action midfielder with an eye for a goal. Teams from much more professional leagues offered her contracts, including clubs in Belgium, Sweden and Finland, but Gillian always turned them down. She loved the Belles, even though she knew she'd always have to work a second job to pay the bills.

Gillian was quickly called up to the England team, and it wasn't long before she was their most influential player. She made her debut at just 18 in a 3–1 win over Ireland and was never out of the team after that.

At a time when female players all had to work side jobs, just about every one of them was forced to use up their holidays whenever they had to travel abroad for an England game or a tournament. Luckily for Gillian, it was different. The owner of the warehouse was a massive football fan, and he always let her take time off for big games without docking her pay!

One of her most historic moments came in 1988 when she played—and scored—in the first-ever women's football match at the original Wembley Stadium. Several years later, she starred in England's first-ever World Cup game in 1995 while also scoring their first-ever World Cup goal!

In between all of these massive milestones*, Gillian had the honour of captaining her country. She did so for most of the nineties, and when she finally did hang up her boots, she had played for England 119 times. Even though she was a defensive player, often anchoring a back five, she still managed to score 30 goals for her country.

Gillian needed all of her battling spirit in 2005 when she was diagnosed with breast cancer. It was a long road to recovery, but she got there. Soon after, Gillian was back at the warehouse, managing the construction line she used to have to work on!

She went into management for a while in the early 2000s, taking over the Hartlepool United ladies' team, but it wasn't really for her.

Gillian was given her MBE in 2021 while still managing the warehouse, where she continued to work at the time of this book being written. With so much success on the pitch, it's a shame that such a legend has been forced to work two jobs to make ends meet when she should be enjoying her retirement from the game she helped put on the map.

Still, we will never forget what Gillian Coultard achieved. Without her, the women's game might still be considered an amateur sport, and that would be a real shame.

NIKITA PARRIS

TEAMS

EVERTON
2011–2015
APPS – 38, GLS – 12

↓

MANCHESTER CITY
2015–2019
APPS – 72, GLS – 37

↓

OLYMPIQUE LYONNAIS
2019–2021
APPS – 35, GLS – 21

↓

ARSENAL
2021–2022
APPS – 18, GLS – 1

↓

MANCHESTER UNITED
2022–
APPS – 34, GLS – 12

TROPHY CABINET

EUROS	X1
WSL	X1
FA CUP	X2
FA LEAGUE CUP	X2
CHAMPIONS LEAGUE	X1

ENGLAND STATS

CAPS	GOALS
71	17

BIOGRAPHY

BORN	10TH MARCH 1994
POSITION(S)	RW / ST
STRONG FOOT	RIGHT
RETIRED	STILL PLAYING
HEIGHT	5 FT 4 IN (1.62 M)

Much like Lucy Bronze, Nikita Parris was still playing when this book was written, so she is far from done creating her legacy*. Already a highly successful player, Nikita still has her best years ahead of her, so who knows how many more special moments she'll create for both club and country.

A dynamic* forward, Nikita has been compared to forwards such as Ian Wright and Gabriel Jesus in that she never gives defenders a second to relax. Finishing seems to come naturally to her, and she has scored goals wherever she's been. At one point, she was the WSL all-time leading scorer, and she was named the Football Writers' Association Women's Footballer of the Year in 2019.

Nikita Parris was born in Toxteth, Liverpool, on the 10th of March, 1994. She grew up in a very sporting family, but things weren't easy. Nikita's father left home when the kids were small, and their mother, Jo, had to work three jobs just to pay the bills. Because of this, Nikita and her siblings grew up fast, but they always had sports to keep them together.

One of the sports the family loved apart from football was boxing, and Nikita's older sister Natasha is actually a world champion boxer! But it was football or nothing for Nikita, who grew up adoring her hero, Arsenal and Scotland star Julie Fleeting. From the age of six, people around Toxteth were talking about the young Parris girl with the golden touch in front of goal!

Nikita grew up playing football with the boys, but she wanted an all-girls team. There weren't any locally, so she did the only thing she could think of—she started her own! She filled the side with girls from her family, friends and neighbours. They called themselves Kingsley United, and after just one year in the local league, they won it!

In fact, Kingsley United are still a top kids' team today. They even have a plaque on the wall near their home ground dedicated to Nikita, the girl who started it all!

Nikita had dreams of playing for her favourite team, Liverpool, but it was their fiercest rivals who came calling first. Everton, as we've already mentioned, are famed in the women's game for their youth setup. They saw Nikita's talents early and offered her a trial. When Nikita turned 14, Mo Marley (the same legendary coach who spotted Lucy Bronze and many more) enrolled Nikita in Everton's Centre of Excellence.

The step up in level worked wonders for Nikita, and her non-stop energy made her a favourite among her teammates. Nikita was known to be shy at times, but once she trusted someone, she became the life of the party. Her dedication and hard work shone through very early on.

It didn't take long for Nikita to be promoted to the senior team, and she made her debut against Arsenal at just 16. If playing her first game against the best team in England wasn't intimidating enough, her second match was a Champions League game! Nikita wasn't fazed* and scored two goals in a 10–0 hammering of North Macedonian side, FK Borec.

She made three appearances in her second season (2011), which was the first year of the WSL. But it was 2012 when she really burst onto the scene, netting six times in 11 games. Nikita continued to improve each year, and in 2014, she was shortlisted for the Young Player of the Year award while also being named on the WSL Team of the Year. Despite her goal-scoring, Everton struggled and were relegated to WSL 2 at the end of the season.

Nikita knew she'd have to play at the top level if she was ever going to break into the England team. With this in mind, she signed for Manchester City, who had already signed her teammates Toni Duggan and Jill Scott. She also joined up with the likes of Lucy Bronze as City continued their attempts at becoming the best team in England.

She made her England debut in June 2016, coming off the bench and setting up a goal in a 7–0 win over Serbia. Nikita was part of the England team that reached the semifinals of Euro 2017, and she scored a cracker in the 2–1 defeat of Portugal in the group stage.

After several massively successful years at City in which she won the WSL title, the FA Cup twice and a couple of League Cups, Nikita signed for European giants Lyon. In her time at City, she recorded 37 goals in just 72 appearances.

Nikita helped the Lionesses to the SheBelieves Cup in 2019, scoring against the USA along the way. It was the first time England had won the trophy, and it was great preparation for the success that was to follow. That same year, she ended England's World Cup qualifying campaign with six goals, more than any other player.

Her first World Cup goal followed that summer when she netted in a 2–1 win over Scotland. But it didn't all go according to plan. After missing penalties against Argentina and Norway (games England still won), manager Phil Neville took Nikita off penalty-taking duties in the semifinal game against America. Steph Houghton stepped up and missed, and England crashed out after a 2–1 defeat.

Following the tournament, Nikita was reinstalled as first-choice penalty taker.

Her time in France was massively successful, and in her three years at Lyon, Nikita won the lot. She returned to England when Arsenal signed her for a club-record fee, but it didn't really work out. A year later, she joined Manchester United.

Nikita was part of the Lionesses who won the 2022 Euros. Despite only making a few sub appearances, she still managed to get on the pitch for the final in front of a massive 81,192 people at Wembley Stadium. Those are the types of memories that last a lifetime!

Nikita's work rate isn't confined to the football pitch. She does a ton of charity work, including setting up the NP17 Football Academy, an organisation that helps struggling students in her hometown of Liverpool.

Apart from that, she has always fought for equality in sport and continues to do so.

She's a legend already, so who knows where Nikita Parris will be ranked by the time she retires? At just 29, she has plenty of years left to play!

ALEX
GREENWOOD

TEAMS

EVERTON
2010–2014
APPS – 43, GLS – 1
↓
NOTTS COUNTY
2015
APPS – 14, GLS – 1
↓
LIVERPOOL
2016–2018
APPS – 32, GLS – 4
↓
MANCHESTER UNITED
2018–2019
APPS – 18, GLS – 4
↓
OLYMPIQUE LYONNAIS
2019–2020
APPS – 11, GLS – 0
↓
MANCHESTER CITY
2020–
APPS – 73, GLS – 4

TROPHY CABINET

EUROS	X1
FA CUP	X1
FA LEAGUE CUP	X1
CHAMPIONS LEAGUE	X1
D1 FEMININE	X1
TROPHEE DES CHAMPIONNES	X1
COUPE DE FRANCE	X1

ENGLAND STATS

CAPS	GOALS
90	6

BIOGRAPHY

BORN	7TH SEPT 1993
POSITION(S)	CB / LB
STRONG FOOT	LEFT
RETIRED	STILL PLAYING
HEIGHT	5 FT 6 IN (1.67 M)

Again, we have one of the players on this list who is still playing and in her prime, too. Alex Greenwood is one of those defenders that every fan and manager wants in their team. Not only is she solid at the back, but she is a danger going forward, especially from set-pieces. She has won everything at club level, including the WSL title, the FA Cup, the League Cup and the Champions League.

Born and raised in the Merseyside town of Bootle, Alex was a phenom from very early on. In fact, she was spotted and signed up by Everton when she was just 6, enrolling in their youth development program. It was quickly noted that she would probably be an England international one day, given how she seemed to make the ball do what she wanted with her left foot.

Her rise through the Everton ranks was rapid, and she was soon signed up on a pro contract when she turned 16. She made her first team debut soon after, playing in a 6–0 win over Faroe Islands' club KÍ in the Champions League. A few days later, she scored her first senior goal, a penalty against FK Borec in that 10–0 hammering that also saw Nikita Parris net two!

So impressive was Alex in her first season at Everton that the management weren't concerned about letting starting left-back Rachel Unitt sign for Birmingham, as they felt Alex was ready to step in. And step in she did, quickly becoming one of the most-talked-about defenders in the WSL.

Her impressive first full season saw her called up to the England Under-19s squad that travelled to Turkey for the 2012 Championship. She rounded it all off by being named the FA Young Player of the Year.

With players such as Alex and Nikita Parris in the team, Everton should have been a growing force. Instead, they were relegated in 2014 (as we covered in the Nikita Parris section). Much like Nikita and several other Everton players, Alex knew she needed to leave if she wanted to fight her way into the England squad for the 2015 World Cup. She signed for Notts County on a two-year deal.

Those two years with Notts County ended up being only one. When Alex's childhood team, Liverpool, wanted to sign her, she didn't hesitate. It was her dream come true. But sometimes dreams don't work out, and even though she played an impressive 32 games for Liverpool in two seasons (scoring four goals from defence), she was released at the end of her contract.

With her England place pretty secure, Alex decided to try a new project and joined up-and-coming Manchester United. The Red Devils had only just been formed, and Alex would have to start in the WSL 2, but she wanted a challenge. She was instantly named captain, and in her first match, United beat Liverpool 1–0 in the League Cup! It was sweet revenge on the team that had released her that summer!

A fantastic first year at United was completed when she led the team to the WSL 2 title and promotion to the top flight.

Her performances alerted Europe's best, and Lyon signed her in 2019, where she teamed up with Lucy Bronze among other stars. In her one season in France, Alex won the quadruple!

This was followed by the SheBelieves Cup victory and then the 2019 World Cup that summer. England performed brilliantly, with Alex scoring against Cameroon in the knockout stage. England went out in the semis, but a team was being built that the public could feel was special.

At club level, she was snapped up by Manchester City after her highly successful year with Lyon. She was still there at the time this book was written and has had several wonderful years there, winning the FA Cup and the League Cup, beating her old club, Everton, in the former.

Although she was part of the Lionesses team that won the 2022 Euros, she only played a minor role on the pitch. Still, she was an important member of the squad and came home a champion. At the World Cup the following year, Alex was used in all seven games as England switched to three-at-the-back. It meant Alex could play as a left-sided centre-back, where her skill on the ball going forward was priceless. By the end of the tournament, she was being hailed as one of the best defenders in the world.

England lost in the World Cup final, but the Lionesses

did themselves proud. In a moment that summed up Alex Greenwood's battling spirit, she suffered a severe head wound during the final, with everyone watching expecting her to come off. After lengthy treatment on the pitch, where the physios patched her up, she played on after refusing to be subbed!

Alex Greenwood is a celebrity in Bootle, where plaques and murals dedicated to her can be seen around town. In truth, she is loved all over the nation, and that image of her refusing to come off as her team battled to win the World Cup will go down in football history.

A true hero and a woman with the heart of a Lioness! They don't come much better than Alex Greenwood!

MARY EARPS
MBE

TEAMS

LEICESTER CITY
2009–2010
APPS – 0
↓
NOTTINGHAM FOREST
2010–2011
APPS – 4
↓
DONCASTER ROVERS BELLES
2011–2012
APPS – 27
↓
BIRMINGHAM CITY
2013
APPS – 11
↓
BRISTOL ACADEMY
2014–2015
APPS – 28
↓
READING
2016–2018
APPS – 34
↓
VFL WOLFSBURG
2018–2019
APPS – 4
↓
MANCHESTER UNITED
2019–
APPS – 94

TROPHY CABINET

EUROS	X1
FRAUEN-BUNDESLIGA	X1
DFB-POKAL	X1
WOMEN'S FINALISSIMA	X1
SHEBELIEVES CUP	X1
ARNOLD CLARK CUP	X2

ENGLAND STATS

CAPS
48

BIOGRAPHY

BORN	7TH MARCH 1993
POSITION(S)	GOALKEEPER
STRONG FOOT	RIGHT
RETIRED	STILL PLAYING
HEIGHT	5 FT 8 IN (1.73 M)

Some people would say that Mary Earps is the greatest keeper in the world. Others would think she is the greatest of all time. Whatever the case may be, she is certainly in there with a shout of both claims.

Outside of football, Mary is a very successful businesswoman, with her clothing range MAE27 becoming a must-have brand. Also, she has appeared on several TV shows, including A League of Their Own. Along with her charity work and the fact that she is still playing in the prime of her football career, it's fair to say that Mary is a very busy woman indeed!

Born on the 7th of March, 1993, in West Bridgford, Nottingham, Mary grew up with a passion for goalkeeping. They say that keepers are a unique bunch, and Mary is no different. Only someone who is a bit quirky would want footballs kicked at them for 90 minutes every Saturday, right?

Mary attended The Becket School in Nottingham, and it was here at the age of 10 that she got her first taste of being a goalie. Like a lot of keepers, it was a position nobody else wanted to play in. Mary gave it a go and instantly became addicted.

After that, Mary was between the sticks any chance she could get, playing for her school's team, West Bridgford FC (her local team), and in the parks and pitches around her estate. But her studies never suffered, and she would later earn a degree in information management and business studies from Loughborough University.

After several teams scouted her as a kid, Mary ended up choosing Leicester City and signed for their youth team. She rose up through the ranks, and she was quickly promoted to the first team as cover for starting keeper Leanne Hall. Mary never made a senior appearance there, and her hometown club, Nottingham Forest, snatched her up when she was still just 17.

Appearances were slim at Forest, too, and Mary became frustrated. She was still a teenager, but she also knew how good she was and wanted first-team football. After four appearances for Forest in her first season, she left and signed for the legendary Doncaster Belles in time for the inaugural* WSL season.

Again, Mary found herself on the bench, but it wasn't long before she got her chance halfway through the season. At 18, she stepped up and nailed down her spot like a boss. She was a starter, and Mary hasn't looked back since.

In fact, she was called up to the England Under-19 squad for the 2012 Under-19 Championship in Turkey and quickly nailed down the number 1 spot in that team, too. Her performances in the tournament brought her a lot of praise, and she was soon being talked about as the future senior keeper.

And she didn't have to wait long for her first call-up. A

string of injuries to the team's goalies meant that Mary was brought into the England squad for the World Cup qualification match against Montenegro in April 2014. Although she wasn't brought off the bench, the experience meant a lot, especially at such a young age.

Her first senior cap came a couple of years later, in a friendly against Switzerland. Mary kept a clean sheet in a 4–0 win, and the nation could see the birth of a true Lioness right in front of their eyes.

Back in the WSL, Mary played for a couple of clubs before a glamour move to Wolfsburg in Germany. While there, she won the domestic double (2018–19) and felt that she was ready to take on a more challenging experience. That challenge was joining Manchester United, who had just been promoted after being formed the previous year. Mary joined up with fellow future Lioness legend Alex Greenwood!

Mary's journey from promising goalkeeper to England's true number 1 was complete when Sarina Wiegman took over as manager in 2021. Wiegman instantly named Mary as her starting goalie, and the rest, as they say, is history! Mary's first game under her new manager was an 8–0 thumping of North Macedonia!

The following year was unreal for Mary Earps, Sarina Wiegman and the rest of the Lionesses. That was the summer of the unforgettable 2022 Euros when the English women achieved what the men's team never has—they won the European Championship. It took them much less time to do it, too!

Mary was fantastic in the tournament, and her performances convinced thousands of young girls all over Britain and beyond that they wanted to be goalkeepers when they grew up. England took home the ultimate prize, and the Lionesses became household names. Not only that, but women's football as a whole was on the map like never before.

The Lionesses followed up their success by beating the mighty Brazil in the Finalissima*.

The 2023 World Cup should have been a special moment for Mary, but it was stained by the behaviour of shirt manufacturer Nike. With World Cup fever sweeping across England, the players' shirts went on sale in sports shops across the country. Nike decided that there would be no call for Mary Earp's jerseys, so they didn't make any!

The public was furious, and Mary took to social media to say how disappointed it made her. Nike backtracked so quickly that they nearly tripped over themselves! Soon, Mary's shirts were being stocked, and the whole lot of them sold out in minutes!

Mary played every second of England's World Cup campaign, where they reached the final. She famously saved a penalty in that game with England trailing 1–0. Sadly, the game ended that way, and England just missed out on the biggest prize in football.

On a personal level, 2023 was a massive success. Mary won the World Cup Golden Glove, England's Player of the Year, came fifth in the Ballon d'Or voting, and was named the BBC Sports Personality of the Year. But she would have swapped it all for her team winning the World Cup. That's just the type of person she is. She's a team player and a born winner.

Mary Earps was appointed her MBE in 2024, and at 30, she still has many years ahead of her. Who would bet against her getting her hands on that World Cup medal she wants so badly when the Lionesses try again in 2027?

ALEX SCOTT
MBE

TEAMS

ARSENAL
2002–2004

↓

BIRMINGHAM CITY
2004–2005
APPS – 15, GLS – 2

↓

ARSENAL
2005–2009
APPS – 72, GLS – 6

↓

BOSTON BREAKERS
2009–2011
APPS – 55, GLS – 1

↓

ARSENAL
2012–2018
APPS – 76, GLS – 6

TROPHY CABINET

WSL	X1
WOMEN'S PREMIER LEAGUE	X5
FA LEAGUE CUP	X3
FA CUP	X7
CHAMPIONS LEAGUE	X1

ENGLAND STATS

CAPS	GOALS
140	12

BIOGRAPHY

BORN	14TH OCT 1984
POSITION(S)	RB / RW
STRONG FOOT	RIGHT
RETIRED	2018
HEIGHT	5 FT 4 IN (1.63 M)

Many players on this list have worked hard for equality in women's football and LGBTQ+ rights, but not many have done as much as Alex Scott. Not only a fantastic footballer who could play right-wing as naturally as her preferred right-back, Alex is someone who has battled endlessly to promote the women's game.

Although she played for Birmingham and the Boston Breakers, Alex is most known for her three spells with Arsenal and her fine career with the Lionesses.

Alexandra Scott was born on the 14th of October, 1984, in Poplar, East London. The girl who would grow up to be inducted into the English Football Hall of Fame in 2019 had a very tough childhood. She was physically abused by her father, and so were the rest of her family.

Such an upbringing could easily make a person bitter, but Alex isn't built that way. In fact, she donated all of the money made from sales of her 2022 autobiography, How (Not) to be Strong, to help women affected by domestic abuse. If angels are real, then Alex is certainly one of them.

Remember, if you or anyone you know is suffering abuse at home or in school, never be afraid to speak up. Alex Scott did, and she was so brave to do so.

Alex attended Langdon Park School as a kid, playing for the boys' side when she could. She also ran out for her local teams but had to move to an all-girls team when she hit her teens. She originally played right-wing, and when Arsenal scouts spotted her at 8, that's the position she believed to be her best. It wasn't until she was switched to defence later on that she realised her true calling!

While still in the Arsenal youth team, Alex was called up to the England team that flew to Canada to play in the 2002 FIFA Under-19 Women's World Championship. She not only travelled with the squad but played a key role in the tournament. England played well, reaching the quarter-finals, where they lost to the hosts.

She spent a decade in Arsenal's youth system but decided to leave when she was 19, as competition for places in the Gunners' first team was high. Alex would have broken into the first team eventually, but she wanted her career to progress. She joined Birmingham in 2004 and helped them finish fourth in her first season.

That year, Alex showed unbelievable growth. Not only did she become a regular at Birmingham, but she also made her senior England debut against Holland!

Despite Birmingham's successful season, the team fell into financial trouble and was forced to sell their best players. Alex was probably the best in the side, and when Arsenal came calling, she felt she was ready to return as a starter.

In her first season back in London (2005–06), Arsenal won the domestic double! If that wasn't enough, Alex and the Gunners won the quadruple the following year! That quadruple included the Champions League, which was a very special moment, as Arsenal became the first British team to win it.

Alex was a key player for England throughout her career, playing in four separate European Championships, including the heartbreaking 2009 tournament when England lost to Germany in the final. She was also part of three World Cup squads. At the 2015 World Cup, she and England got some form of revenge on Germany when they beat them in the third-place playoff.

After four years with Arsenal (her second spell) and near-total domination of the English game, Alex decided she wanted a fresh challenge. A new, more professional league had just started in America, and she felt that it could be the experience she wanted. She signed for the Boston Breakers in 2009, where she was joined a few months later by England teammate Kelly Smith!

Alex stayed in America until the WPS folded in 2012 before returning to her beloved Arsenal. Again, she was joined by Kelly Smith.

A couple of years after rejoining, Alex was named Arsenal captain, a role she held until her retirement in 2018. Her international retirement had come a year before, on the 2nd of September, 2017, when she hung up her boots after playing for her country an astonishing 140 times. She is one of the most-capped players in the history of English football.

Following her fantastic career, Alex moved into punditry*. She has commentated on games for Sky Sports, TNT Sports (formerly BT Sports), and many other channels. She also appeared on several TV shows, including Match of the Day, Soccer AM and Goals on Sunday.

Alex Scott is one of the most recognisable and talented Lionesses to ever play the game. Given how much work she's done for equality in the women's game, she is surely one of the most important, too.

CAROL THOMAS MBE

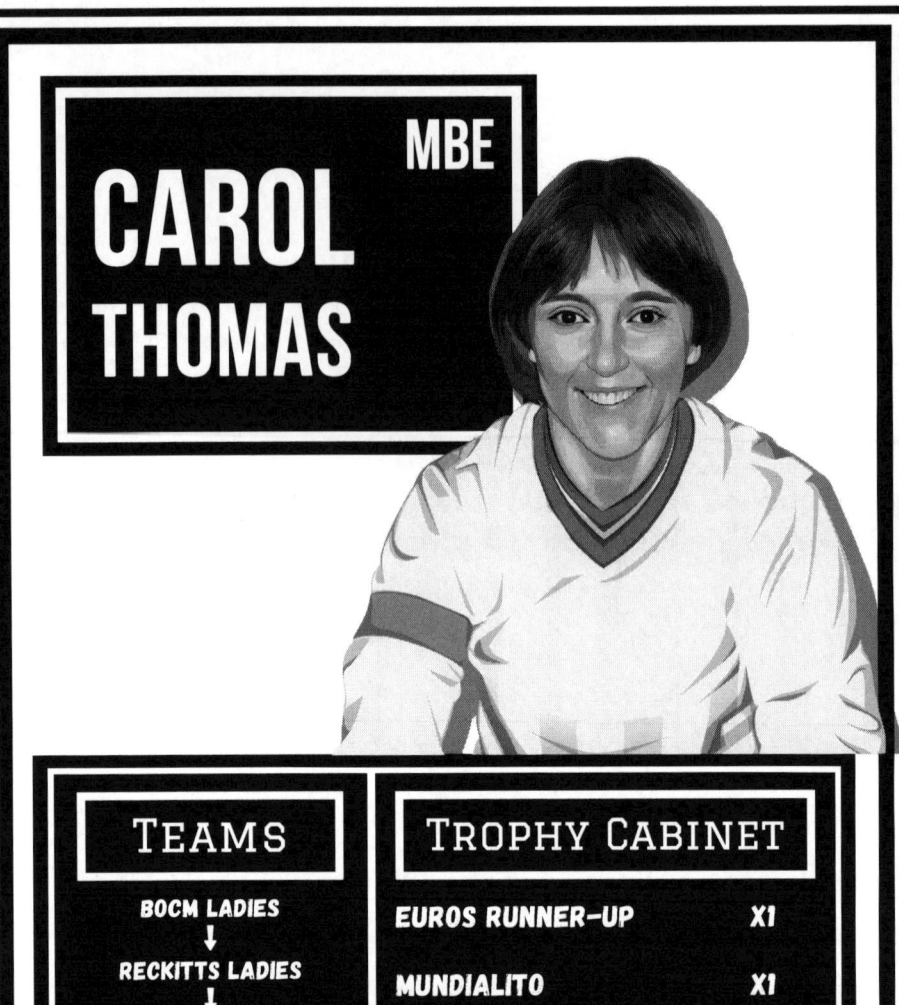

Teams

BOCM LADIES
↓
RECKITTS LADIES
↓
HULL BREWERY LADIES
↓
PRESTON LADIES
↓
CP DONCASTER LADIES
↓
ROWNTREES F.C. LADIES
↓
AFC PRESTON
↓
BRANDESBURTON LADIES

Trophy Cabinet

EUROS RUNNER-UP	X1
MUNDIALITO	X1
PONY HOME INTERNATIONALS	X1

England Stats

CAPS
56

BIOGRAPHY

BORN	5TH JUNE 1955
BIRTHPLACE	HULL
POSITION(S)	RB / MIDFIELDER
RETIRED	2009
HEIGHT	N/A

One of the most impressive things about Carol Thomas is that her career lasted longer than most of the players on this list have been alive! In her 43-year playing career (yep, you read that correctly—she played for 43 years!), Carol Thomas did more for the women's game than most. Sadly, there isn't an awful lot known about her career, which is a terrible shame, given how important she is to football.

Carol also spent an impressive nine years as England captain, and she was the first female player to reach 50 caps.

Born on the 5th of June, 1955, in Kingston upon Hull, Carol grew up surrounded by football. Her father was actually a pretty good player himself and had a part-time career at the amateur level. He formed his own club when Carol was a kid and filled it with other semi-pro players, including a lot of his brothers. Carol used to love going to watch her dad and uncles play and dreamed of one day being a footballer herself.

Her passion to play the game she loved when she grew up massively increased when, at age 11, she tuned in to watch England lift the 1966 World Cup. Seeing Bobby Moore and Bobby Charlton perform miracles at Wembley brought hopes of her doing the same one day, but most people laughed when she told them about it.

Anyone who doubted her was quickly left with egg on their face. In a moment that would seem impossible today, Carol made her competitive debut at the age of 11 when she played for British Oil and Cake Mills! Remember, the rest of the team was made up of adults!

At the time, organised women's football was banned in Britain and would be until 1971. These "factory games"* were the only way for the ladies to play a decent standard of football against each other.

Despite these so-called bans, Carol played regardless, often joining in her brothers' matches at school. She was so good that most of the other boys hated seeing her lace up her boots. At first, she wanted to be a winger, but after seeing how much enjoyment she got from tackling, she switched to a more defensive role.

As she got older, she found the Hull Brewery Ladies team and signed up. In her three years there, Carol's talents came to the attention of some reporters who did a story on her. Still, she was never paid for playing and had to work full-time at Northern Dairies, a small company in her hometown.

Unlike a lot of factories and warehouses at the time, Northern Dairies actually supported Carol's England career. She showed her loyalty to them and the English game by turning down professional contracts in countries such as Italy and New Zealand. She wanted to always be available for her nation, and it was this loyalty that led to her becoming the first female player to reach 50 caps.

Carol enjoyed spells at clubs such as Preston, Doncaster and Hull City. While at Hull, she often trained with the men, with their manager wishing the rules could be changed to let Carol play in the first team!

Early on in her England career, she asked for the chance to study for her coaching badges*. The Football Association agreed, and she later became one of the first fully qualified female football coaches. She achieved all of this not long after making her England debut in a 2–0 win over France.

After only five first-team appearances, Carol was named England captain, and all before she turned 21! She held onto the armband for the rest of her international career, during which time she only missed one match.

She led the England side out at the 1984 European Championship, where England lost on penalties in the final. It was an agonising way to lose, but it helped shape the way women's football was seen in Britain. There was still a long way to go, but that tournament was a big step forward.

Several other major steps were taken with Carol as captain of England. She oversaw the first time the women's team played in a men's top-division stadium. There was also the first time the women's team played outside of the country when they travelled to Japan. And in the seven major tournaments in which she captained England, the team reached at least the semis in all of them!

In 1985, Carol retired from football at the age of 30 to give birth to her first child. In her 56 appearances for England, she captained the side 51 times! Shockingly, she came out of retirement in 1993 (she was 38!) to play for AFC Preston, a team she had helped create.

What's even more impressive is that she continued playing until 2009, when she finally properly retired at the age of 54!

Carol has remained extremely active, even into her sixties. Since her retirement, she has completed the National Three Peaks Challenge, where people attempt to climb the peaks of the highest mountain in each of England, Scotland and Wales in a 24-hour period. She has done the Coast to Coast Walk, a 190-mile trek from one coast of Northern England to the other. And she has climbed the Andes, the Himalayas and the Atlas Mountains!

Throughout all of this, Carol has held down several jobs, including school lunchtime supervisor and delivering post, a position she held until 2013. Currently, she runs a successful Twitter account dedicated to women's football before the WSL, and she is an ambassador for Hull City.

Some of you will never have heard of Carol Thomas until now, and that's a shame, but the important thing is that now you know. Without her, it's safe to say women's football wouldn't be anywhere near where it is today. She is the meaning of the word legend!

CASEY STONEY MBE

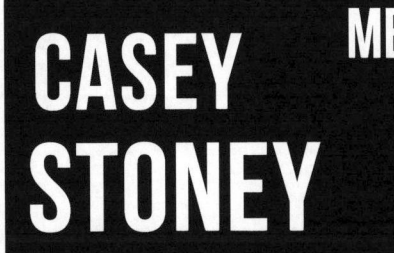

Teams

ARSENAL
1999–2002
↓
CHARLTON ATHLETIC
2002–2007
↓
CHELSEA
2007–2011
↓
LINCOLN
2011–2013
APPS – 38, GLS – 1
↓
ARSENAL
2014–2016
APPS – 39, GLS – 5
↓
LIVERPOOL
2016–2018
APPS – 14, GLS – 1

Trophy Cabinet

WOMEN'S PREMIER LEAGUE	X2
FA CUP	X4
FA LEAGUE CUP	X1
NATIONAL LEAGUE CUP	X4
FA COMMUNITY SHIELD	X3
FA INTERNATIONAL PLAYER OF THE YEAR	X2

England Stats

CAPS	GOALS
130	6

61

BIOGRAPHY

BORN	13TH MAY 1982
BIRTHPLACE	BASILDON
POSITION(S)	DEFENDER
RETIRED	2018
HEIGHT	5 FT 9 IN (1.74 M)

Casey Stoney has done a lot to promote women's football, and she was one of the first openly gay players to push for more LGBTQ+ rights. But first and foremost, she was a fantastic player who could play anywhere across the back. Her leadership skills made her a winner, something she has continued into her coaching career.

Apart from captaining her country, she also wore the armband for Team Great Britain at the 2012 Olympic Games in London. She is currently head coach of the San Diego Wave, having managed Manchester United from their formation in 2018 until 2021.

Casey was born in Basildon, Essex, on the 13th of May ,1982. From the moment she could walk, she was kicking a ball. Her parents knew they had a special player on their hands early on when the neighbourhood boys used to complain that Casey was just too good for them. She played for the local boys' teams until she was 12, when the rules meant she had to switch.

It worked out well for her, though. By then, Chelsea scouts had spotted her playing and offered her a trial. She blew them away, and they signed her up, but she was soon poached* by Arsenal, who always wanted the best young players in the country on their books.

Her first taste of international football came in 2000 when she came on as a sub against France. She even made the original 30-player list for the 2001 Euros despite being so young, but she didn't make the final 20. Still, she was only 19. There was plenty of time left for her to become an England legend!

By the early 2000s, Casey had started to break into the Arsenal team, but she wasn't playing as often as she would have liked. After a couple of years, she asked for a move, and Charlton signed her in the summer of 2002.

She made her first England start that same year in a match against Norway and impressed with her versatility. She could play in any defensive position, which meant that she was often called up for England squads, as there would usually be a spot for her somewhere on the pitch.

Casey's first season with Charlton was astonishing. She captained them to their first-ever FA Cup final, and two years later, they won the League Cup. They followed this up in 2005 by winning the FA Cup for the first time, beating Chelsea 1–0 in the final. More success came the following year when they won another League Cup, this time beating Arsenal!

Her first England goal came in a 4–0 win over Portugal in March 2005, so when she was called up for the 2005 Euros, she expected to play plenty of games. It didn't work out that way, and she spent the whole tournament on the bench. The rejection affected her so much that she genuinely considered retiring from international football.

When Charlton's men's team got relegated from the Premier League in 2007, the women's team were disbanded*. Casey was gutted, and she spoke out about how unfair it all was. Why should the women's team—who were so successful—be punished because the men's team failed?

With no club, the biggest teams in Europe all tried to sign her. Casey chose Chelsea, the team she had signed for as a kid before Arsenal poached her.

The 2007 World Cup was the opposite of the Euros two years before, as Casey played every minute. She slotted in at left-back for the whole tournament, but England went out in the quarter-finals after a 3–0 loss to the USA.

During the 2008–09 season, Chelsea manager Steve Jones retired. In what was a huge surprise, the board asked Casey to take over as player-manager. She was still in her 20s! It was a successful period, and it confirmed Casey's belief that she could coach full-time when her playing career ended.

She managed the team until the end of the season, and when Chelsea hired Matt Beard before the 2009–2010 season, it was only because Casey had recommended him!

Casey was a major part of the England team that reached the Euro 2009 final, and she continued her form into the World Cup two years later, when she once again started every game. When the quarter-final against France went to penalties, Casey stood up and scored her spot kick, but it wasn't enough, and England crashed out.

Following England's exit, Casey was named as captain, which she claimed was the best moment of her life.

She followed up the World Cup by captaining Team GB at the 2012 Olympics, and a year later, she became the first-ever female member of the Professional Footballers' Association management committee. But 2013 wasn't all perfect, as she captained England to a disastrous 2013 Euros when they finished bottom of their group.

When Hope Powell was replaced as England manager a couple of years later, new manager Mark Sampson immediately took the captaincy from Casey, naming Steph Houghton in her place. After that, several injuries and a lack of playing time saw her career wind down. Still, she was called up for the England squad for the 2015 World Cup, but she only played a bit part.

The same thing happened at the 2017 Euros, and Casey played her final game for England a few months later in a friendly with France, the team she'd made her debut against! She retired with 130 caps for her country.

Casey moved into coaching after retiring from playing, and she is quickly becoming one of the best. Would any of us be surprised if she coached the Lionesses one day? Here's hoping she does!

RACHEL YANKEY OBE

Teams

ARSENAL
1996–2000
APPS – 47, GLS – 8
↓
LAVAL DYNAMITES (LOAN)
1996
APPS – 25, GLS – 10
↓
FULHAM
2000–2004
APPS – 15, GLS – 6
↓
BIRMINGHAM CITY
2004–2005
APPS – 13, GLS – 7
↓
NEW JERSEY WILDCATS
2005
APPS – 29, GLS – 5
↓
ARSENAL
2005–2016
APPS – 151, GLS – 43
↓
NOTTS COUNTY (LOAN)
2016
APPS – 5, GLS – 0

Trophy Cabinet

WSL	X2
WOMEN'S PREMIER LEAGUE	X7
FA CUP	X11
NATIONAL LEAGUE CUP	X6
CHAMPIONS LEAGUE	X1
USL W-LEAGUE	X1

England Stats

CAPS	GOALS
129	19

BIOGRAPHY

BORN 1ST NOV 1979
BIRTHPLACE LONDON
POSITION(S) LW / CF
RETIRED 2016
HEIGHT 5 FT 4 IN (1.63 M)

Mostly known for her two spells with Arsenal, where she won six Premier Leagues, two WSL titles, nine FA Cups, four League Cups and a UEFA Cup, Rachel Yankey is one of the most successful players in the women's game. In four years with Fulham, she also won the Premier League, two FA Cups and two League Cups.

Rachel was a fantastic attacking player who could drift out wide or play through the middle, and she put fear into every defender she came up against. In an England career in which she won 129 caps, she was her country's all-time leading appearance-holder for a stage. When she reached her 100th cap, she became the second woman in history to do so after Gillian Coulthard.

Rachel was born in London on the 1st of November, 1979. She spent her childhood there and played organised football from an early age, usually with the boys. When she was 8, Rachel was told she couldn't play on the boys' teams anymore, so she shaved her head and told people her name was Ray. It worked for a couple of years before her secret was revealed, and she was forced to switch to the girls' team.

As a teen, she joined the prestigious* Mill Hill United. It was here that she was spotted by Arsenal's scouts, and she soon signed youth terms with the Gunners.

After moving up the ranks for a few years, Rachel was sent on loan to Canadian side Laval Dynamites, where she made her competitive debut at just 16. By the time she returned to London, she felt like she was ready to force her way into Arsenal's first team.

Her senior England debut came soon after when she played against Scotland in a 4-0 win in August 1997. She was only 17.

Off the pitch, Rachel was becoming a national celebrity. She was often seen on the cover of football magazines or on chat shows. Her fame, mixed with her talent on the pitch, helped promote women's football in a way that hadn't been done before, making her one of the most important figures in British sport.

In her first spell with Arsenal, she made 47 appearances in four years, scoring eight goals. In that time, she won every domestic trophy available. A move to Fulham in 2000 followed, which quickly brought even more success. But her transfer to Fulham was important for one very big reason. Rachel Yankey became the first woman in the history of the English game to be registered as a professional.

Rachel had a fantastic 2002, winning the domestic treble with Fulham. She spent a year in America and, of course, won the league while she was with the New Jersey Wildcats. When it was time to return to England, there was only one club Rachel wanted to join... her beloved Arsenal!

Despite the high number of caps Rachel racked up for England, it wasn't all plain sailing. In fact, she was left out of the squad for the 2009 Euros. To make matters worse, she was dropped for the 2011 World Cup qualifiers against Malta and Turkey. Some pundits believed this had something to do with her playing in the States at the time, which seemed to be proved correct when she was brought back into the England squad soon after rejoining Arsenal.

England coach Hope Powell began to use Rachel as the main point of her attack, and following another treble (this one with Arsenal), her career took on a whole new level. When England played their return fixture against Turkey in the World Cup qualifiers, Rachel not only played this time, but also captained the team! Oh, and it just so happened to be her 100th cap for England! And, double-oh... she scored in a 3–0 win!

After fearing that she wouldn't even make the England squad for the 2011 World Cup, Rachel was now a guaranteed starter by the time the tournament began. She scored in a 2–0 win over eventual-winners Japan in the group stage before that heartbreaking defeat on penalties to France.

The following year, Rachel equalled Gillian Coulthard's caps record when she played in a 4–0 thrashing of Slovenia. A few days later, she won her 120th cap in a 3–0 win over Croatia, making her the most-capped female player at the time. When she surpassed Peter Shilton's record in 2013, she became the most-capped English player (both male and female) of all time!

Rachel Yankey retired from international football following England's disappointing 2013 Euros, with an unbelievable 129 caps to her name. She played on with Arsenal for a few more years, finally calling it a day in December 2016.

Since hanging up her boots, Rachel continues to be involved in the sport she loves so much. She works in local schools, coaching and teaching the kids how to play the game in the right way, and has even tried her hand at TV, hosting the CBeebies kids' programme, Footy Pups!

To play for your country 100 times is something most players can only dream of. Rachel Yankey did it on 129 occasions! With a record like that, it can't ever be denied that she is a legend and a true Lioness!

FARA WILLIAMS MBE

Teams

CHELSEA
2000-2001
↓
CHARLTON ATHLETIC
2001-2004
↓
EVERTON
2004-2012
APPS - 122, GLS - 70
↓
LIVERPOOL
2012-2015
APPS - 35, GLS - 9
↓
ARSENAL
2016-2017
APPS - 22, GLS - 2
↓
READING
2017-2021
APPS - 67, GLS - 25

Trophy Cabinet

WSL	X2
FA CUP	X2
NATIONAL LEAGUE CUP	X1
CYPRUS CUP	X3

England Stats

CAPS	GOALS
177	40

BIOGRAPHY

BORN	25TH JAN 1984
POSITION(S)	MIDFIELDER
STRONG FOOT	RIGHT
RETIRED	2021
HEIGHT	5 FT 5 IN (1.64 M)

Now, if playing for your country 129 times is epic, then imagine doing it 177 times! Yep, you read that right. Fara Williams earned an astonishing 177 caps for her country during her career. If that doesn't make her a Lioness legend, then nothing will!

Fara earned each and every one of those caps due to her laser-sharp technique and her ability to score goals from midfield. She was one of the players to star at the 2012 Olympics for Team GB, and throughout her career, she managed to win the Young Player of the Year award, the Players' Player of the Year award and the International Player of the Year award (twice).

Born in Battersea, London, on the 25th of January, 1984, Fara spent her early childhood playing on the concrete pitches near her home. She could be found there from the moment she finished school until it was too dark to see the ball. Money was tight at home, and her mother had to save for months to buy Fara her first pair of boots.

Fara was spotted by Chelsea's scouts early on, and she signed youth terms with them before she was even 10. At 12, she was playing (and bossing it) in their Under-14s. Somehow, Fara managed to concentrate on her game and her studies despite everything that was happening at home.

Things had gotten so tough for Fara's mother that she regularly had to send her daughter to live with her grandmother. Fara was bounced between the two homes, and she often went hungry. At the age of 17, Fara found herself living on the streets. Sometimes she was lucky and slept on a friend's couch or in a hostel, but things were really bad.

Shockingly, she made her England debut as a sub in a game against Portugal while she was living in a hostel. She was still 17, which shows how highly her talents were rated, yet she couldn't afford a place to stay. Would that happen in the men's game? No, we think not. Fara's story is one of the reasons why the women's game is still so far behind and more support is needed.

On the pitch, she was shining. On her first start—the return fixture against Portugal—Fara scored a stunning free kick in a 3-0 win.

Her first season at Chelsea was immense. She scored 30 goals from midfield, and her reputation soared. Never before had a kid broken through in the women's game and made such a splash so early on. She was instantly snapped up by Charlton, and in her first season there, she was voted their best player and won the Young Player of the Year award.

The 2002-03 season was heartbreaking, and Fara missed most of it with a back injury. She returned the following year and quickly found her form again. Sadly, Charlton just missed out on the FA Cup and the league, which they lost by a single point. They did win the League Cup, though, so it was still a successful season.

By 2005, Fara was a regular starter for England. She played all of the Lionesses' games at the Euros that year and scored a penalty against Denmark. Following the tournament, her form continued to improve, and in 2007, she won the International Player of the Year award for the first time.

A shock move to Everton followed, but it ended up being a great decision. Fara became a club legend there, spending eight wonderful years displaying her silky skills and quickly earning the nickname "Queen Fara"! She is still adored by Everton fans despite having played her last game for them in 2012.

The 2008–09 season saw Everton winning the League Cup, thrashing Arsenal 3–0 in the final. They agonisingly lost the league on goal difference, but Fara still picked up the Players' Player of the Year award.

During that season, Fara was unplayable at times. In one memorable game for England in May 2008, she scored a hat trick of long-range worldies in a World Cup qualifier against Belarus. Each strike was a goal-of-the-season contender, and if you've never seen them, then look the game up on YouTube. You are in for a treat!

She was one of England's best players as they tore it up at Euro 2009, but the team came unstuck against a wily German side in the final. Despite the pain of losing, the Lionesses had done more for the women's game than they ever could have imagined, as more people than ever were tuning in.

At the end of 2009, Fara won her second International

Player of the Year award. She was offered some big-money contracts by teams in the USA and beyond, but Fara stayed with Everton. Her loyalty was rewarded when they lifted the FA Cup in 2010, beating Arsenal in extra time in what has been described as one of the greatest finals ever. So, you know what to do... search the game online and get watching! But only after you have finished reading this book, of course!

Fara's 2011 was another personal milestone. She was the top scorer at the 2011 World Cup, even though England crashed out in the quarters. She followed this up with her 100th cap, a 1–0 win over Switzerland in which Fara scored the only goal.

She joined Everton's rivals Liverpool in 2012, and she instantly raised them to a new level. They won the league in 2013 and 2014!

A year later, she started for England at the 2015 World Cup, where they finished third. It was England's best-ever performance at that level and wasn't matched until the 2023 final loss to Spain. That tournament also saw England's first win over Germany, which was a massive step forward.

The next few years saw her career winding down, and moves to Arsenal and Reading followed. Fara played on until 2021 when she retired as England's most-capped player.

Fara's marriage to Everton teammate Amy Kane was big news at the time, and their pride and refusal to be anyone but themselves helped promote LGBTQ+ rights in football and beyond, something which Fara has always fought hard for. She was a fighter on the pitch and is a fighter off it, too.

England's most-capped player? Enough said!

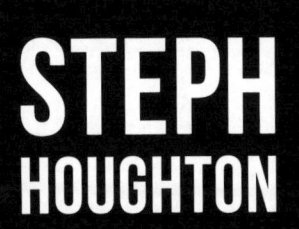

STEPH HOUGHTON
MBE

TEAMS

SUNDERLAND
2002–2007
APPS – 61, GLS – 24

↓

LEEDS UNITED
2007–2010
APPS – 47, GLS – 9

↓

ARSENAL
2010–2013
APPS – 39, GLS – 7

↓

MANCHESTER CITY
2014–
APPS – 137, GLS – 17

TROPHY CABINET

WSL	X3
FA CUP	X5
NATIONAL LEAGUE CUP	X1
FA LEAGUE CUP	X7
CYPRUS CUP	X3

ENGLAND STATS

CAPS	GOALS
121	13

BIOGRAPHY

BORN	23RD APRIL 1988
POSITION(S)	CENTRE-BACK
STRONG FOOT	RIGHT
RETIRED	STILL PLAYING
HEIGHT	5 FT 9 IN (1.74 M)

We have heard Steph Houghton mentioned a few times already in this book, and with good reason! She has helped shape the women's game into what we know today, and her trophy cabinet is as stuffed as a Christmas turkey! Steph's versatility made her a coach's dream, and at different points in her career, she's played up front, in midfield, and in defence!

But her most outstanding achievement is probably the fact that she managed to play for her country 121 times despite several serious injuries throughout her career. She always came back just as strong, which is nearly impossible to do unless you are Superwoman! In a way, Steph kind of is!

Born Stephanie Houghton in Durham on the 23rd of April, 1988, Steph grew up wanting to prove something to the world. She often recalls how the local boys used to tease her by claiming football was a "man's game," even after she had just left them all on their backsides on the pitch. They probably said these things because she'd just shown them up.

Still, she played every chance she got—for her school's team in Durham, her local parks and the organised kids' teams. She was spotted by Sunderland early on and signed up for their youth programme, initially as a striker.

She was quickly brought into the England youth teams, rising through the grades rapidly. The same thing happened at club level, and Steph was thrown into the Sunderland first team as a teenager. She took off like Usain Bolt, helping the team win promotion to the Premier League in 2006 and then winning the Young Player of the Year award in her first season in the top flight.

Her full England debut wasn't long in coming, and she came on as a 73rd-minute substitute in a 6–0 demolition of Russia in March 2007. A few days later, she was a starter and performed brilliantly in a 1–0 win over the old enemy, Scotland.

Her rapid rise was stalled when the first of her severe injuries struck just before the 2007 World Cup when she broke her leg and missed the tournament. Sadly, the same thing happened right before the 2009 Euros, only this time it was a cruciate ligament* injury.

Leg breaks and cruciate ligament injuries have been known to end careers on their own. Steph suffered both of them in a two-year period and still bounced back. That tells you all you need to know about her character.

Despite her injury problems, Steph was one of the 17 female players given contracts by the FA. Rachel Yankey was one of the others. It was a huge step forward for the women's game.

After five years with Sunderland, Steph felt she needed to make a step up. She was their best player by a mile and wanted to play for a team that matched her talent.

Arsenal and Leeds battled it out for her signature. She chose Leeds and spent three years there before moving to Arsenal, so both teams saw the best of Steph!

In her time with both clubs, she won everything there is to win in England.

When City emerged in 2013 and started splashing the cash, Steph was one of many future legends that they snapped up. Steph spent the rest of her career there, winning the WSL, three FA Cups and four League Cups.

Her first proper shot at a major tournament for England came at Euro 2013. Unfortunately (as you've seen earlier in the book), this was the famous (or infamous) tournament when the Lionesses finished bottom of their group. Following the disastrous Euros, manager Mark Sampson took the captaincy off Casey Stoney and gave it to Steph.

Steph captained England at the 2015 World Cup, scoring her first World Cup goal, a lovely finish against Norway in the last 16. In the quarters, she was named Player of the Match against powerhouses Canada, a game England won to reach their first-ever World Cup semifinal!

Steph's 100th England cap came in a game against Sweden on the 11th of November, 2018, and led England to the World Cup a year later. Once more, they lost in the semis, but the Lionesses were well and truly being built into one of the best teams on the planet. Women's football in Britain had never been so popular.

Steph retired from international football in 2021, having played for the Lionesses an impressive 121 times. In March 2023, she was given the Freedom of the City of Sunderland, one of the most prestigious honours a person can get.

If she showed up at a local park today, we wonder if the boys would tell her football is a man's game. We're willing to bet that they wouldn't. In fact, it would be a dream come true for them to share the pitch with a living legend!

SHEILA PARKER
MBE

TEAMS

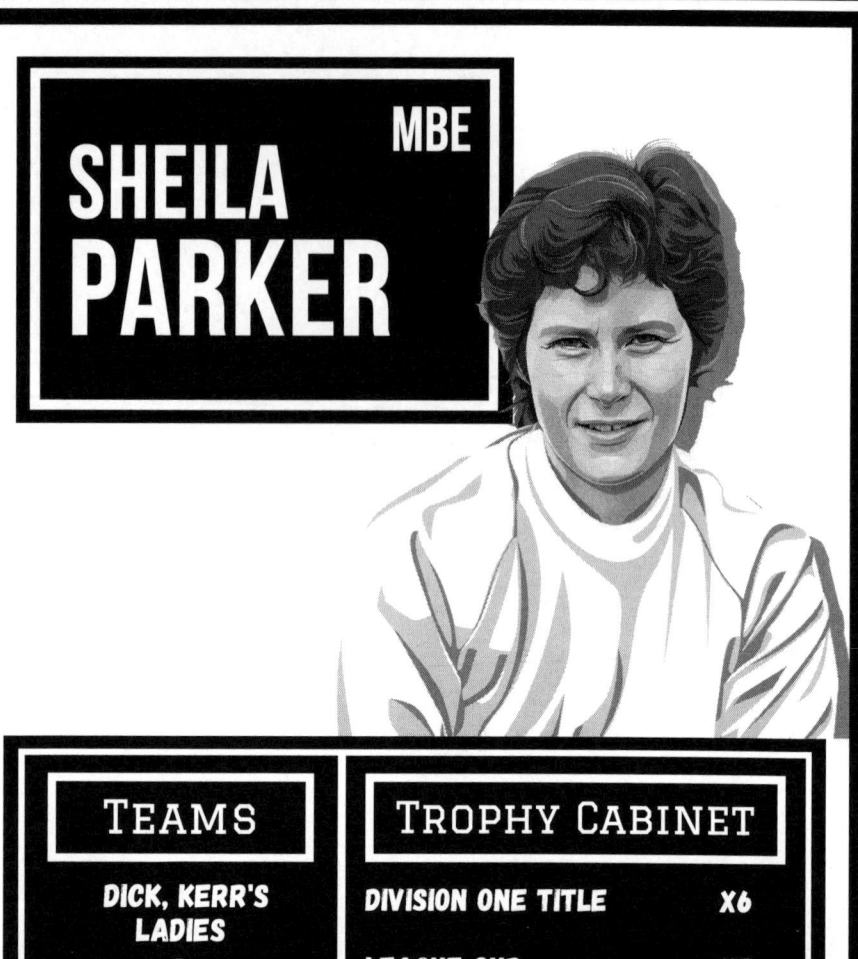

DICK, KERR'S LADIES
↓
CHORLEY
↓
FODENS
↓
PRESTON
↓
ST. HELENS

TROPHY CABINET

DIVISION ONE TITLE — X6
LEAGUE CUP — X5
FA CUP — X1

ENGLAND STATS

CAPS	GOALS
33	5

BIOGRAPHY

BORN	1947
POSITION(S)	DEFENDER
STRONG FOOT	N/A
RETIRED	1984
HEIGHT	N/A

This entry is important for many reasons, with the main one being that Sheila Parker was the first-ever captain of England's women's team. There is probably no better introduction than that!

There is a reason why Sheila Parker is known as the "woman who started it all": She basically did, at least in terms of finally forcing people to take women's football seriously in Britain. It's fair to say that without her, there would be no WSL or Lionesses as we know them today.

Being born in the late forties and growing up in the fifties meant that Sheila had little to no option to play organised football. Even joining in with the boys in the local park was frowned upon. In her hometown of Chorley, the idea of a girl wanting to grow up to be a footballer was laughed at. It took everything Sheila had in her to keep believing, and we are all glad she did!

After much searching, she finally found a team she could play for around the time she turned 13. The Dick, Kerr Ladies side were one of the only organised women's teams at the time, but it was also a team filled with adults. When little skinny Sheila showed up for training after school, the other women wondered how she'd cope. She not only stood her ground but ran rings around the adults!

And she wasn't just training with the first team. Sheila made her competitive debut at 13!

After a few years with Dick, Kerr Ladies, she moved to Chorley Ladies. Despite always being the best player on the pitch, there was hardly ever a chance for this to happen. Sometimes her team could go months without a game, and the international scene was no different. England barely ever played.

In fact, throughout her career, and despite the fact that Sheila was relatively injury-free, she only got the chance to represent England 33 times.

A versatile defender with an eye for goal, it is said that Sheila was years ahead of her time in the way she looked after herself and how she played on the pitch. She was a modern defender before there was such a thing as modern defending! She had an eye for goal and could beat a player when needed.

A couple of special moments occurred when Sheila was 24. In 1971, the FA finally lifted the ban on women playing organised international football, and they created the first women's international team. The FA hired Eric Worthington, who instantly named Sheila as England's captain, making her the original. The OG. The GOAT. The woman who started it all.

In her and England's first game as a legit team, the Lionesses beat Scotland 3–2 after coming from two goals down. History had been made, and Sheila Parker was at the forefront*.

Sheila held onto the captaincy for the rest of her

international career, and she led the team out for the first-ever home international championships.

One of Sheila's most treasured moments on a football pitch came in 1974 when she led Fodens Ladies FC to the FA Cup. This achievement was unbelievable for many reasons, the main one being that the team they beat, Southampton, had never lost a cup match in the three years since the FA Cup had been in existence. Secondly, the team Sheila won it with, Fodens, had only been a team for a few years. Before that FA Cup run, Edwin Foden, Sons & Co. was basically a truck and bus manufacturing company that had a women's team on the side!

This shock would be the same as Salford or Halifax beating Manchester City in the final of the men's FA Cup today.

Her performances led to a move to Preston, who were one of the only women's teams that even came close to being professionally run. Being surrounded by players who took the sport as seriously as she did helped Sheila to reach new heights.

Another one of her achievements that is so unreal that it seems not to make sense came a year later when she scored 51 goals in a 14-game season on the way to the title. Remember... Sheila was a defender!

By the mid-seventies, she was the most famous women's player in history, and that Preston team was becoming unstoppable. In total, Sheila won six Division One (later the Premier League, then the WSL) titles, five League Cups and that heroic FA Cup with

Fodens.

But it's the breakthroughs she made for the women's game that will forever remain her legacy. She made it so the likes of Steph Houghton, Casey Stoney and basically any player on this list could become heroes. Without people like Sheila Parker in the world, nothing would ever move forward in the women's football world.

How would she have fared if she played today? We would imagine she would still be one of the best players on the pitch. Can you name a team that wouldn't want a 51-goal-a-season defender in their squad? We didn't think so!

ELLEN WHITE MBE

Teams

CHELSEA
2005-2008
APPS - 48, GLS - 21
↓
LEEDS CARNEGIE
2008-2010
APPS - 24, GLS - 17
↓
ARSENAL
2010-2013
APPS - 38, GLS - 11
↓
NOTTS COUNTY
2014-2016
APPS - 24, GLS - 6
↓
BIRMINGHAM CITY
2017-2019
APPS - 26, GLS - 23
↓
MANCHESTER CITY
2019-2022
APPS - 56, GLS - 20

Trophy Cabinet

EUROS	X1
WSL	X2
FA CUP	X3
NATIONAL LEAGUE CUP	X1
FA LEAGUE CUP	X4
CYPRUS CUP	X1
SHEBELIEVES CUP	X1

England Stats

CAPS	GOALS
113	52

BIOGRAPHY

BORN	9TH MAY 1989
POSITION(S)	ST / LW
STRONG FOOT	RIGHT
RETIRED	2022
HEIGHT	5 FT 7 IN (1.70 M)

The woman who has scored the most goals for her country doesn't need much more build-up than that stat, but we'll do it anyway!

Ellen White has not only scored more goals than anyone else for her country, but she's scored the most World Cup goals, too. In fact, in the three World Cups she's played in, the Lionesses have never done worse than reach the quarter-finals, and they reached the semis in two of them. That Euro 2022 win was her swansong*, and she retired as one of the most natural finishers ever to play the game.

Born on the 9th of May, 1989, in Aylesbury, Buckinghamshire, Ellen White showed huge promise early on. Blessed with the ability to finish with ease, she dominated her school's boys' team and continued to do so until she was kicked off at age 9 for being a girl. It hurt, but that was also the same year that scouts from Arsenal saw her play and asked her to join their youth setup, so it wasn't all doom and gloom!

She stayed with Arsenal until she was 16 when Chelsea poached her, and she left without having made a first-team appearance. She didn't have to wait long at Chelsea, and as soon as she made her senior debut, she never looked back. In her three seasons with Chelsea, Ellen was their top scorer every year!

A move to Leeds followed, but her maiden* season was cut short when she suffered the first of many serious injuries. This one was cruciate ligament damage. It kept her out for most of the campaign, and she only managed four games. Still, in those four games, she banged in five goals!

Her second season was better, and she helped Leeds to the League Cup final, where they beat Everton 3–1 to lift the trophy. Ellen scored two of the Leeds goals and picked up the Player of the Match award.

Sadly, as we've seen so often in this book, the women's game isn't very well funded, even today. Fifteen years ago, it was even worse, and despite the success Ellen had helped Leeds achieve, the club was forced to fold when they couldn't make enough money. Ellen and her teammates had to look for new clubs.

Ellen made her England debut in 2010, scoring an injury-time goal in a 3–0 win over Austria. It was the first of many goals she would score for the Lionesses.

With no club, Ellen had her pick of teams to sign for, and she chose the best in England—Arsenal. She won the treble in her first year and two more leagues in the following couple of seasons. She also added several cups to her trophy haul in three unbelievable years with the Gunners.

After only a few games for England, she was selected for the squad that travelled to Germany for the 2011 World Cup. She scored her first World Cup goal in the group stage game against Japan, with Rachel Yankey adding the second. England lost on penalties in the quarter-finals.

After her time at Arsenal, Ellen joined Notts County, but another horrific injury threatened to end her career. ACL injuries* are one of the worst a footballer can have, but Ellen recovered in such a short space of time that she shocked her doctors. Somehow, she got herself fit in time for the 2015 World Cup, in which she helped the Lionesses finish third.

Her time at Notts County was uneventful for Ellen's standards, and after a brief spell with Birmingham, she joined that up-and-coming Manchester City team we've heard about so much in this book! Her first game for City was in the Champions League, and she played fantastic throughout the season.

Ellen carried her form into the 2019 World Cup, a tournament in which she caught fire. She scored in the opening group game against Scotland, then added two more in the final group game against Japan. Her fourth goal came in the last 16 tie against Cameroon, and her fifth in the 3–0 defeat of Norway in the quarter-finals. In the semis, she netted the equaliser against America and had another disallowed before winning the penalty that Steph Houghton unfortunately missed.

Ellen ended the World Cup as the joint top scorer and as England's all-time leading World Cup goalscorer.

That World Cup brought women's football in Britain to a new level of popularity, which was proven when England played Germany at Wembley soon after. A crowd of 77,768 turned up to cheer them on, and it broke the record for the highest attendance at a

Lionesses game.

Ellen became the WSL's all-time leading scorer on the 7th of February, 2021, when she overtook the great Vivianne Miedema. Later that year, on the 27th of November, she made her 100th appearance for England in a 1–0 win over Austria. She scored the only goal of the game! Well, what else would we expect from such a legend!

Of course, her proudest moment came at Euro 2022. By then, Ellen was one of the team's veterans, and her experience proved priceless. She started all six games, scoring two goals along the way as the Lionesses made history. It was and is one of the greatest sporting moments in the history of British sport, and it was all because of those brilliant women.

Ellen White retired after the Euros, despite her seemingly being in the prime of her life. Some people wonder if she'd stuck it out for another year, could she have been the difference between England winning the 2023 World Cup and that agonising defeat to Spain? Given how devastating Ellen was in front of goal, who's to say that she wouldn't have found an equaliser that night!

KAREN CARNEY MBE

Teams

BIRMINGHAM CITY
2001–2006

↓

ARSENAL
2006–2009
APPS – 54, GLS – 28

↓

CHICAGO RED STARS
2009–2010
APPS – 38, GLS – 3

↓

BIRMINGHAM CITY
2011–2015
APPS – 50, GLS – 12

↓

CHELSEA
2015–2019
APPS – 36, GLS – 10

Trophy Cabinet

WOMEN'S PREMIER LEAGUE	X3
FA CUP	X5
CHAMPIONS LEAGUE	X1
NATIONAL LEAGUE CUP	X1
FA COMMUNITY SHIELD	X1
CYPRUS CUP	X3
SHEBELIEVES CUP	X1

England Stats

CAPS	GOALS
144	32

BIOGRAPHY

BORN	1ST AUG 1987
POSITION(S)	RM / LM
STRONG FOOT	RIGHT
RETIRED	2019
HEIGHT	5 FT 4 IN (1.62 M)

The woman who became known as the "Wizard," Karen Carney, certainly earned her nickname. She could score from midfield, and her vision was exceptional, while she had an almost magical ability to find space. She was part of the Arsenal team that won the quadruple in 2007, and she played at four World Cups and four Euros for the Lionesses.

Since her retirement, she's become one of the most recognisable pundits on TV, and she has appeared on every major sports channel. Her 144-cap haul for England was the second-most at the time, and she can easily be considered one of the best players to ever pull on the shirt.

Karen was born on the 1st of August, 1987, in Birmingham. She grew up in Hall Green and attended St Ambrose Barlow Catholic Primary School and then St Peter's Secondary School. Her father was a firefighter, and her mother worked at Sainsbury's. Karen claims that her humble upbringing helped her to always appreciate the little things in life. She never took her footballing career for granted*.

While playing for her local side as a kid, Karen was spotted by Birmingham scouts and signed up for their youth system at 11. Some of her teammates as she progressed up the ranks included future stars, Eniola Aluko and Laura Bassett. Karen's rise through the youth teams was rapid, and she made her senior debut at just 14!

After a few years of first-team football, Karen was already one of Birmingham's best players. She won the Young Player of the Year award in 2005 and then again in 2006. In between, she made her England debut, coming off the bench and scoring in a 4–0 defeat of Italy. In doing so, she became the youngest debutant during Hope Powell's time as England manager.

Karen was a shock inclusion in the 2005 Euros squad, given her age, but she quickly changed opinions when she scored a last-minute winner against Finland in the group stage. That goal made her a national star and brought her to the attention of the world's biggest clubs.

Arsenal came in for her in 2006, and she knew she couldn't turn down the chance to join the team that had dominated English football for so long. In Karen's first season with the Gunners, they won that historic quadruple! Karen played nearly every game, scoring 13 goals from midfield.

In the four years she spent at Arsenal, her numbers increased every season. She just kept getting better and better.

When the new so-called more professional league started up in America in 2009, Karen was one of the many English players tempted by the chance to get paid a decent wage while playing the sport they love. She played two seasons with the Chicago Red Stars, who had just employed her old assistant coach at Arsenal, Emma Hayes. Her time in America wasn't as successful as she'd hoped, but the experience was priceless.

She returned to England and joined Birmingham City, her hometown club. In her first season (the first WSL season), she helped Birmingham to a second-place finish. One of her standout moments was a beautiful goal against her old team, Arsenal, to win the game.

Throughout all of this, she remained one of the Lionesses' most important players. Her consistency was one of her best assets, and it also meant that she won her 100th cap when she was just 27. She became the youngest player in history to do so while also doing it in front of a record crowd for a Lionesses match.

Karen helped Birmingham to the FA Cup in 2012, scoring the winning penalty after a 2-2 draw and picking up the Player of the Match award in the process. The following season, Birmingham finished second again, with the always-consistent Karen playing every minute!

At the 2015 World Cup, Karen scored in the group games against Mexico and Columbia, with England eventually finishing third.

One of her crowning moments came in 2015 when she became the first woman in history to be inducted into the Birmingham City FC Hall of Fame. Sadly, that was the same year she left her beloved club when Emma Hayes took charge of Chelsea and re-signed her favourite player!

Karen was called up for the 2019 World Cup, and she announced before it began that it would be her last. She was to retire after it. England reached the semifinals but couldn't quite go all the way. Karen retired from club football around the same time, leaving behind a wonderful legacy.

Throughout her career, Karen always continued to educate herself, earning several degrees and life skills such as business and sports science. She is a proud vegan who claims that she never would have been so consistently fit if it hadn't been for her strict diet.

She retired a few years before the Lionesses won the Euros, but that takes nothing away from her legendary status. Karen Carney is most definitely one of the greatest English players of all time.

FRAN KIRBY

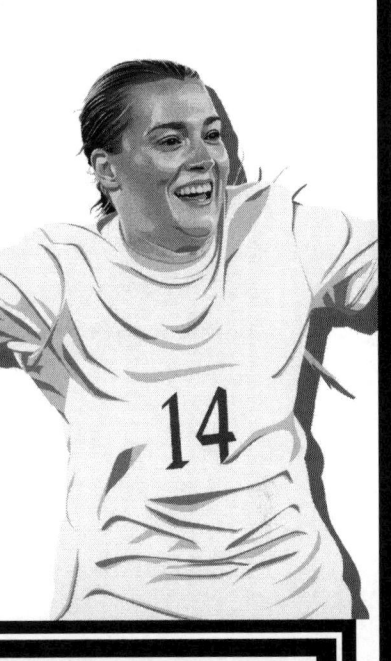

TEAMS

READING
2012–2015
APPS – 43, GLS – 68

↓

CHELSEA
2015–
APPS – 108, GLS – 62

TROPHY CABINET

EUROS	X1
WSL	X5
FA CUP	X4
FA LEAGUE CUP	X2
FA COMMUNITY SHIELD	X1

ENGLAND STATS

CAPS	GOALS
69	19

BIOGRAPHY

BORN	29TH JUNE 1993
POSITION(S)	CAM / RW
STRONG FOOT	RIGHT
RETIRED	STILL PLAYING
HEIGHT	5 FT 2 IN (1.57 M)

Phil Neville once described Fran Kirby as the best number 10 in the game. With her ability to drift between the lines, assist and score, it's hard to argue with that statement.

At just 30, Fran has plenty of time left to continue her rise to the top, and in the eight years or so that she's been at Chelsea, she has helped them become the dominant force in English football. In this timeframe, Fran has also become the club's record scorer.

Born and raised in Reading, Fran was obsessed with football before she even knew what it was exactly. Her mother says that she used to sit Fran with her buggy facing the local pitch so she could watch her older brother playing football with his pals. Another time, when Fran was three, her mother took her to the doctor for a regular check-up. When the doctor tossed Fran a tennis ball to see if she'd catch it, she volleyed it back to him!

At that point, Fran's mother knew her little girl would be a footballer!

As soon as she could run, Fran played football non-stop. On the street, in the park or with local teams—it didn't matter. She just wanted a ball at her feet.

She signed for her hometown club, Reading, when she

was 7 and worked her way up the ranks, making her debut at 16. But a moment that should have been magical was actually a dark time for Fran. A couple of years before, her mother (and biggest fan) died of a brain haemorrhage. Fran hadn't dealt with the grief, and around the time of her breakthrough into the Reading side, her depression worsened.

Before her career had really begun, Fran retired. She was in too dark a place.

After a few months, one of Fran's friends invited her for a five-a-side game in the local gym. Fran went and instantly fell in love with the game again. After some very important counselling, she returned to the Reading team, determined to do it for her mum.

Always remember that sadness, anxiety and depression are real issues that should never be ignored. Never ever be afraid to ask for help if you don't feel okay. It's one of the bravest things a person can do.

In her first full season (2012–13), Fran was the Premier League Southern Division's leading scorer with a staggering 32 goals in 21 games. Her goals catapulted Reading into the Premier League 2 (now WSL 2), where they finished an impressive third place, mainly due to Fran's 24 goals in 16 games.

Reading knew they had a world star on their hands and made her the first female player in their history to sign a pro contract.

Fran's senior England debut came in June 2014, when she scored a goal in a 4–0 win over Sweden. She followed this up by being named in the England squad for the 2015 World Cup and scored her first World Cup goal in a 2–1 win over Mexico. Her startling performance in that game caused some people in the press to nickname her mini-Messi!

An injury forced Fran to miss the quarter and semifinals, which hurt. But her top performances hadn't gone unnoticed, and Chelsea broke the then-British transfer record to sign her. It was a move that suited Fran, as she was ready to take that next step up.

In her first seasons with Chelsea, they won their first major trophy, lifting the FA Cup. They followed this up very soon after with their second—the WSL title, making it a wonderful double. It was the beginning of a pretty impressive period of Chelsea dominance that would not have happened without Fran in the team.

After playing and scoring at the 2017 Euros, Fran came into the 2017–18 season in top form. She carried it through the year, finishing the season with the Player of the Year award and the Football Writers' Player of the Year award!

During that period of excellence, Fran tore apart a world-class Brazilian team at Wembley. In a game that was seen as a battle of the number 10s (six-time World Player of the Year Marta being the other), Fran ran the show. England manager Phil Neville claimed afterwards that there had only been one winner!

Fran was diagnosed with pericarditis* in November 2019, and when doctors told her she might never play again, she was devastated. Amazingly, Fran not only beat it but fought her way back to fitness in time for the Community Shield win over Manchester City on the 29th of August, 2020! She is a true fighter.

In December of that year, her two goals in a 5-0 Champions League win over Benfica moved her past Eniola Aluko as Chelsea's all-time leading scorer with 70 goals. As we mentioned earlier, Fran has many years left at the top. If she stays with Chelsea for that time, who knows how far ahead she'll be on the charts when she hangs up her boots?

She was a massive part of the Chelsea side that won the domestic quadruple in 2021 and then the England squad that won the 2022 Euros. Sadly, like so many current players on this list, she missed the 2023 World Cup due to injury.

Fran has always been proudly and openly gay. She is a big supporter of LGBTQ+ rights and does a lot of work to promote mental health issues.

Fran Kirby's journey to football began that day when she was 3 and volleyed a tennis ball back to her doctor. Well, at 30 years old at the time this book was written, that journey still has a long way to go!

LEAH WILLIAMSON

TEAMS

ARSENAL
2014–
APPS – 137, GLS – 8

TROPHY CABINET

EUROS	X1
WSL	X1
FA CUP	X2
FA LEAGUE CUP	X3
FINALISSIMA	X1

ENGLAND STATS

CAPS	GOALS
43	4

BIOGRAPHY

BORN	29TH MARCH 1997
POSITION(S)	CENTRE-BACK
STRONG FOOT	RIGHT
RETIRED	STILL PLAYING
HEIGHT	5 FT 7 IN (1.70 M)

Our second-to-last entry is the youngest player on the list at just 26. Still, in her relatively short career, Leah Williamson has captained Arsenal, won the WSL title and several cups, and, most impressively, captained the Lionesses to the 2022 Euros.

This is a book dedicated to the greatest and most important female England players, so not having the championship-winning captain in it would be a crime! But Leah isn't only here because of that one tournament. She's on this list because she's one of the best ball-playing defenders to ever pull on the shirt.

Born on the 29th of March, 1997, in Milton Keynes, Leah grew up a passionate Arsenal fan. But not all of her family were Gooners. In fact, the house was split between Arsenal and Spurs, London's two biggest rivals. Still, it was Arsenal or nothing for Leah, which probably explains why she's spent her whole career there thus far.

Leah was so football-mad as a kid that she constantly sent letters to Arsenal and the England team in the hopes that she could be a mascot and walk out onto the pitch with her heroes. Her dreams came true, and in 2006, she stepped out onto the Emirates turf with the Arsenal men's team, holding Theo Walcott's hand. The framed photo of the two of them together is still one of her prized possessions.

She also got her wish with England, walking out with Kelly Smith, who was captaining the Lionesses for the game. Leah would end up being Kelly's teammate and then, later, the captain of the national team!

Leah first trained with the Rushden & Diamonds youth programme, but when her coach left to join the staff at Arsenal, he took Leah with him. She signed for the team she'd always adored when she was 9! It's fair to say that she hasn't looked back since!

She made her senior debut for the Gunners the day she turned 17 (2014), coming on in the 81st minute for Rachel Yankey. Leah ended her first season as an FA Cup winner.

Initially a defensive midfielder, Leah continued to play there for large parts of her early career. She was called up to the England squad in November 2017, but only to be in and around the first team's training sessions. The staff wanted her to get a feel for it, knowing that it was only a matter of time before she became a regular.

The 2017–18 season was one of Leah's best. She played nearly every minute of the season as Arsenal won the WSL title. That was the season that she made the switch from centre-midfield to centre-back. Her skill on the ball helped Arsenal in transition, and they became one of the most feared counter-attacking teams in the league, while Leah quickly became one of the most natural ball-playing defenders in the world.

By 2019, she was also a regular for the Lionesses, and she played an important role in the team that won the SheBelieves Cup. But for some reason, when the

World Cup rolled around that summer, manager Phil Neville began to use her sparingly*. If he'd played her as his main centre-back and used her throughout the tournament, then England would probably have fared better.

Following the World Cup, Leah began to start for England again. She scored her first international goal in a 3-2 win over Cameroon on the 12th of November, 2019, which was a special moment for her and one she'll never forget. The same could be said for her at club level, as Leah had started to captain the Arsenal team more and more.

Leah's leadership skills have always been one of her best attributes, and this was proven when she captained her country at just 24 years of age in a World Cup qualifier against North Macedonia. Less than a year later, she was named as permanent captain, taking over from Steph Houghton. It was Steph who actually recommended Leah for the role.

Of course, as we've mentioned, she was captain of the Lionesses for that Euro 2022 victory, meaning she was the first person to get her hands on the trophy. She followed it up by captaining England to victory against Brazil in the Finalissima.

Sadly, she missed the 2023 World Cup with (you guessed it) an injury. At times, it can feel like fate or luck or something else that just didn't want the Lionesses to win that World Cup. How else could they have had such bad timing with injuries!

While she was injured, Leah could have sulked. For

any player, missing a World Cup must be devastating. But Leah Williamson's not the type to waste time feeling sorry for herself. Instead of moping around the house, she spent her recovery mastering the piano and even ended up performing with the BBC Concert Orchestra!

Despite her young age, Leah Williamson has done an incredible amount of charity work and activism* already. She's a proud supporter of the LGBTQ+ community, and she travels to countries devastated by disasters, disease, war and famine to lend a hand whenever she can. She has written children's books, and she has even spoken at the United Nations, becoming the first female footballer to do so.

Talk about keeping yourself busy! What a legend!

BETH MEAD
MBE

TEAMS

SUNDERLAND
2011–2016
APPS – 82, GLS – 66

↓

ARSENAL
2017–
APPS – 117, GLS – 41

TROPHY CABINET

EUROS	X1
WSL	X1
WOMEN'S PREMIER LEAGUE	X2
NATIONAL LEAGUE CUP	X1
FA LEAGUE CUP	X2

ENGLAND STATS

CAPS	GOALS
53	32

Both of Beth's Premier League titles were after it was demoted to the level 2 of English football

BIOGRAPHY

BORN	9TH MAY 1995
POSITION(S)	RIGHT-WING
STRONG FOOT	RIGHT
RETIRED	STILL PLAYING
HEIGHT	5 FT 4 IN (1.63 M)

Perhaps the most natural finisher England has produced, Beth Mead can score goals from anywhere. Despite only being 28 when this book was written, she's already broken many records for goals and assists, so who knows where she'll be on the charts when she retires!

Beth became the first female footballer to win the BBC Sports Personality of the Year award when she collected it in 2022, paving the way for the likes of Mary Earps to follow. She was the top scorer at the 2022 Euros while leading the assists chart and winning Player of the Tournament, too.

Bethany Mead was born on the 9th of May, 1995, in Whitby and raised in the nearby village of Hinderwell. She claims that Hinderwell—which only has a population of 2,000—was nothing more than a fishing village with a post office, a couple of pubs and a lot of sheep! Still, she adored the place and still does.

She first kicked a ball when she was 6. Her mother, who was exhausted from trying to keep up with Beth's endless energy, found out where the local kids played football and let Beth loose in the hopes that she would run off some of it. Beth fell in love with the sport and would sprint to the pitch every day she could to join in.

But it wasn't just football Beth loved. She excelled in many sports, including netball, cricket, cross-country running and hockey, although nothing compared to football.

When it was time for primary school, Beth couldn't wait to get there and sign up for the team. Unfortunately, there was no girls' team, but Beth didn't hesitate. She joined the boys' team as the only girl and quickly became their best player and captain. In fact, she was so good that other girls in the school started to join.

The Oakridge Community Primary School won the league soon after, with Beth among four girls in the team!

Middlesbrough were the first team to spot her, signing her to their youth development system when she was 9. With money tight and training a good drive away, Beth's mother had to take up a second job to pay for petrol so she could drive her there and back.

When Beth was 13, she played for Middlesbrough's Under-16 team in a match against Sunderland. She scored a hat trick in six minutes, causing the Sunderland coach to instantly approach Beth's mother and try to sign her. Sunderland were a much more professional outfit at the time, and everyone felt it was the right move for Beth's development.

It only took Beth a few years to break into Sunderland's first team, and while still a teenager, she became a regular starter. In her first season, she scored 23 goals in 23 games as she helped Sunderland to promotion. They also shocked the nation by winning the League Cup.

The following season saw another promotion, this one to the WSL. In a fantastic campaign, Beth scored 30 goals in just 28 games. While achieving all of this, she continued to study at university and work in a local bar.

Beth's first match in the WSL came on the opening day of the season, and it was magical. Not only did she score, but Sunderland beat defending champions Liverpool 2–1. Soon after, she scored her first WSL hat-trick against Chelsea.

Now, here's the truly amazing part: A week before that Chelsea game, Beth had flipped her car and rolled it three times when she swerved to avoid hitting a deer, yet she started, scored a hat trick and won Player of the Match!

Beth ended the 2015 season as the league's top scorer, winning the Golden Boot and becoming the youngest player in the history of the women's game to do so at just 20. She was quickly being recognised as a world star, and becoming an England regular was surely just around the corner.

In her five seasons with Sunderland, she guided them to two promotions, the League Cup and scored 66 goals in 82 games. She is widely regarded as Sunderland's greatest-ever player.

Arsenal snapped her up in time for the 2015–16 season while also bringing in Vivianne Miedema. This meant that Beth had to switch positions, moving out to the wing instead of through the middle. It was hard at first, having spent her whole career as a number 9, but she soon adapted. In the end, Beth fell in love with playing out wide, as it gave her a chance to run at defenders and rack up more assists for her teammates.

In her first season with Arsenal, Beth won the second Young Player of the Year award of her career.

Amazingly, her England debut didn't come until April 2018, in a World Cup qualifier against Wales, when she came on as a sub. She started her first match a few days later, banging in a brace* against Kazakhstan.

At the 2019 SheBelieves Cup, Beth scored two absolute worldies, including the winning goal against Brazil. She followed this up by playing a major role in England's 2019 World Cup, where they reached the semis, a game that was watched by a record 11.7 million viewers in the UK.

During the 2021–22 season, Beth entered a record-breaking period with the Lionesses. She scored her first international hat trick in a 4–0 win over Northern Ireland in a World Cup qualifier, becoming the first woman to score an international hat trick at Wembley. She grabbed another hat trick a month later in a record 20–0 destruction of Latvia. Four months later, she bagged four goals in a 10–0 win over North Macedonia.

Following two wonderful goals to turn the game around against Holland, Beth surpassed the great Jimmy Greaves's decades-old record of 13 international goals in a season when she reached 14. In the end, she finished the year with 20 goals and 16 assists in just 19 matches.

We could be wrong, but we're pretty certain that record won't ever be beaten.

Of course, the 2022 Euros was her defining moment. Beth helped the Lionesses to victory with six goals and five assists. She won the Golden Boot and Player of the Tournament and was directly involved in half of England's goals!

When she won the BBC Sports Personality of the Year award at the end of 2022, nobody was surprised. The same thing could be said about her being appointed her MBE. Beth is a genius, and a genius deserves to be recognised.

It goes without saying that she picked up an injury before that cursed World Cup, but at 28, she will be at the height of her career when the next one rolls around. If the Lionesses can keep their best players fit for that summer in 2027, we're betting they will make history and bring football home!

FINAL WHISTLE

So, we hope you've enjoyed our list of legendary Lionesses. Of course, there were so many fantastic players who didn't make the cut, but that's simply because we would have needed hundreds of extra pages to fit them all in! England have produced so many fine footballers over the years, so this list is just the tip of the iceberg.

You might wonder why there are so many MBEs, OBEs and other honours attached to these ladies' names. Well, the answer is quite simple: They've earned them.

Coming up in any professional sport is hard enough. Doing so when the rules are against you and the opportunities don't really exist is nearly impossible. That's why these women are special. It's not just their undeniable talent; it's the struggles they had to go through to even get paid for doing what they do best.

People like Sheila Parker and Gillian Coulthard had to fight for their right to play. They had to come through hatred, sexism, dismissal and so many other horrible things to reach the top, but they never gave up. With each legendary Lioness comes the next one, and more after that. They've had to pave the way for each other throughout the history of the game.

But it all seems worth it when we look at the images of

the Lionesses lifting the trophy at Euro 2022, doesn't it? That moment was special for so many more reasons than the victory itself. It was another massive step forward for women's football in Britain and beyond.

It raised the television ratings and attendance at WSL games. It put people like Mary Earps and Beth Mead in the running for the BBC Sports Personality of the Year award, something a female footballer had never won before. With that exposure comes more viewers and even higher attendance.

Think of Fara Williams still living in a hostel as she scored a free kick against Portugal, and you will see how hard it has been for women to get the same respect as men in football. Remember, that was as recent as 2002, so it's not like it was fifty or sixty years ago. Yes, things have gotten better, but not nearly enough.

By reading this book, you've done your part in promoting the women's game. You've learned more about the Lionesses and the women who started it all, and that's all we can ask. And we hope you've enjoyed yourself along the way!

Now, all that's left for you to do is to decide which player deserves to be top of the list, as your opinion is all that matters when it comes to choosing! Is it Beth Mead or Marieanne Spacey? Maybe it's Casey Stoney? What about "the woman who started it all," Sheila Parker? You see, it's not so easy, is it?

Whether you're a young boy or girl reading this book or even an adult, it's great that you've decided to follow the women's game. It seems like each week the WSL sees an attendance record being broken or viewing figures being smashed, and that's amazing. Compared to where women's football was thirty or forty years ago, it's an astonishing achievement. But as we've mentioned throughout this book, there's a long way to go yet!

But with players like Beth Mead, Mary Earps and Leah Williamson still in the prime of their careers and so many more stars of the women's game producing magic on the pitch, the future is bright. For fans of the Lionesses, the 2027 World Cup can't come quickly enough, and every football fan in the nation will surely tune in to see it unfold.

And that's the beauty of football. It's for everyone. It's the greatest sport in the world. And some of the best players ever to step onto the pitch have been covered in this book.

The England women. The Lionesses.

APPENDIX

CAM - Central attacking midfielder.

CB - Centre-back.

CDM - Central defensive midfielder.

CF - Centre-forward.

LB - Left-back.

LM - Left-midfielder.

LW - Left-winger.

MBE - Member of the Order of the British Empire. One of the highest honours a person can receive in Britain.

OBE - Officer of the Order of the British Empire. An even higher honour than an MBE awarded to a select few who have done incredible things.

RB - Right-back.

RM - Right-midfielder.

RW - Right-winger.

RWB - Right wing-back.

ST - Striker.

GLOSSARY

ACL injury - The anterior cruciate ligament is one of the main ligaments that helps to keep the knee in place. When it's damaged, it's extremely hard to get it back to 100%.

Activism - Trying to make changes to society.

Bilingual - Can speak two languages.

Brace - Two goals in one game.

Coaching badges - The qualifications you need to become a professional coach.

Cruciate ligament - The ligaments that are usually in joints, such as fingers, wrists, knees, etc.

Disbanded - A group or organisation that ends or breaks up.

Dynamic - Full of energy and ideas and constantly changing for the better.

Exodus - A mass exiting of a large group.

Factory games - Football matches that were played between different factories' teams.

Fazed - To "not be fazed" means to stay confident and not falter in pressure situations.

Finalissima - A game played between the winners of the European Championship and the Copa America.

For granted - To take something for granted is to not appreciate something.

Forefront - Ahead of everyone or everything else.

Friends of Fulham - The original team in Fulham before they moved to Wimbledon.

Inaugural - The beginning of or first to something.

Legacy - The reputation a person, team or company, etc. leaves behind when they're gone or finished.

Lopsided - Uneven or off-balance.

Maiden - First of something.

Milestone - A particular achievement or important place in time.

Pericarditis - A serious swelling around the heart.

Poached - To take something, usually in a sly way, but not always.

Prestigious - Highly respected, important or special.

Punditry - Commentating or discussing sports for a TV channel.

Sparingly - To use something not very often.

Swansong - A final moment in a career or life. Usually a big spectacle or event.

Sweeper - A defensive player who sits behind the defensive line and deals with any balls that come into that zone.

Toffees - The Toffees is the nickname of Everton Football Club.

Printed in Great Britain
by Amazon